TEEN
TRAILBLAZERS

"I'VE BEEN ABSOLUTELY TERRIFIED
EVERY MOMENT OF MY LIFE
AND I'VE NEVER LET IT KEEP ME
FROM DOING A SINGLE THING
THAT I WANTED TO DO."

–GEORGIA O'KEEFE

TEEN TRAILBLAZERS

30 FEARLESS GIRLS

WHO CHANGED THE WORLD
BEFORE THEY WERE 20

JENNIFER CALVERT

ILLUSTRATED BY
VESNA ASANOVIC

CASTLE POINT BOOKS
NEW YORK

www.stmartins.com
www.castlepointbooks.com

The Castle Point Books trademark is owned by Castle Point Publications, LLC.
Castle Point books are published and distributed by St. Martin's Press.

ISBN 978-1-250-20020-4 (trade paperback)

Design by Katie Jennings Campbell
Editorial by Monica Sweeney

Our books may be purchased in bulk for promotional, educational, or business use.
Please contact your local bookseller or the Macmillan Corporate and
Premium Sales Department at 1-800-221-7945, extension 5442,
or by e-mail at MacmillanSpecialMarkets@macmillan.com.

First Edition: October 2018

10 9 8 7 6 5 4 3 2 1

CONTENTS

"I ALONE CANNOT CHANGE THE WORLD, BUT I CAN CAST A STONE ACROSS THE WATER TO CREATE MANY RIPPLES."

—MOTHER TERESA

"WE DO NOT NEED MAGIC TO CHANGE THE WORLD, WE CARRY ALL THE POWER WE NEED INSIDE OURSELVES ALREADY: WE HAVE THE POWER TO IMAGINE BETTER."

—J. K. ROWLING

"BE NOT AFRAID OF GREATNESS. SOME ARE BORN GREAT, SOME ACHIEVE GREATNESS, AND OTHERS HAVE GREATNESS THRUST UPON THEM."

—WILLIAM SHAKESPEARE, *TWELFTH NIGHT*

INTRODUCTION

Changing the world sounds like a big, scary endeavor meant for the leaders of countries and political movements. But real change is simple. It happens slowly, a little bit at a time. Change is not an enormous snowball charging furiously down the hill—it's the snowflakes that drift softly onto the mountain. The snowball is nothing without them, and they are nothing without each other.

Even the smallest actions can add up to incredible change. Claudette Colvin (page 79) refused to give up her seat on a bus. Her act of courage inspired the actions of others, and soon the snowball was moving toward the end of the segregated bus system. Emma Watson (page 95) auditioned for a movie and brought to life a beloved book character. Then she realized she could use her fame to help women all over the world, and the snowball started moving toward equality.

But change can happen only when someone imagines that things can be different than they are. Not everyone has the vision to strike out on a new path, or the strength to oppose the people who say it can't or shouldn't be done. Those who do are called *trailblazers*. They set the snowball in motion. And the world needs more of them.

We're lucky today: most women have the freedom and confidence to move in any direction we like. We also have those who came before us as role models. They paved the way. But the girls in this book were often the first of their kind, with no one to look up to but themselves. Mary Shelley (page 39) published the first science fiction novel in history, Mary Pickford (page 59) created the movie star, and Nellie Bly (page 55) pioneered investigative journalism—all in an era when women were told to sit down and be quiet. Society didn't expect much from these girls, so they had to expect more from themselves. Although we've come a long way, there's still progress to be made and paths for new teen trailblazers to forge.

The amazing young women in this book were different from each other in every way—place, time, and social standing. Some had the benefit of supportive parents, or the gift of talent. Others just believed in something greater than themselves. Some set out to change the world, others did it almost by accident. But every one of them was smart, creative, resilient, brave, hopeful, and kind. And every one of them had to overcome obstacles like poverty, sexism, racism, war, and the inescapable specter of fear.

These teenage trailblazers are proof that anyone and everyone can change the world. The stories contained here are just the beginning. When you find someone or something that speaks to you, do what these brilliant girls did, and set out to learn more. Then take one small step in the direction you want the snowball to move. Start today. Start before you're ready. Just start.

CLEOPATRA

THE LAST ACTIVE PHARAOH OF EGYPT

BORN: 69 BC · DIED: 30 BC

- Became queen of Egypt when she was 18 years old
- Brought peace and prosperity to Egypt during her 22-year reign
- Was a brilliant political mind and take-charge leader

> "FOR HER BEAUTY, AS WE ARE TOLD, WAS IN ITSELF NOT ALTOGETHER INCOMPARABLE, NOR SUCH AS TO STRIKE THOSE WHO SAW HER; BUT CONVERSE WITH HER HAD AN IRRESISTIBLE CHARM."

–PLUTARCH, *LIFE OF ANTONY*

Cleopatra made history for her ruthless political tactics, sensational love life, and bold ambition. But these qualities were never without their qualifier: her gender. Those history-making attributes were most commonly assigned to men. They were applauded in men. In a woman, they were considered shocking and unbecoming. Women could be powerful, of course, but society felt (and still feels, in some circles) that their power should be quiet and understated. Cleopatra was neither quiet *nor* understated.

EGYPT: THE SOAP OPERA

For all of its murder, intrigue, and romance, Cleopatra's reign over Egypt could put *Game of Thrones* to shame. But that's how the Romans rolled. (Egypt was part of Rome, off and on.) Family members marrying each other to keep bloodlines pure wasn't uncommon. Nor was murdering those same family members over money or power. What was a little treasonous assassination plot between friends?

Cleopatra was just 18 years old when her father died and she became queen of Egypt. She had 100 years of royal ancestry to live up to, and three ambitious siblings to contend with. One of those siblings, her younger brother, ran her out of the country just three years into her rule. She fled to Syria and began raising up an army against him.

EGYPT UNDER CLEOPATRA

Cleopatra's first priority was always that Egypt flourish under her family's rule. That was her guiding principle in ousting her brother, in captivating Caesar and Antony, and in governing day to day. Although she had a cunning political mind, she was a kind and empathetic queen. When flooding from the Nile ruined food crops, she opened her stores of grain to all of Egypt. Although Greek by birth, she learned and spoke the Egyptian language of her people. For 22 years, she maintained Egypt's independence from Rome and bolstered its economy. Her love affairs are fascinating, but her legacy as a leader and businesswoman is incredible.

At the time, Rome was becoming increasingly combustible thanks to a country-splitting spat between leaders Julius Caesar and Pompey. Pompey sought refuge in Egypt, where Cleopatra's little brother didn't think twice before having him killed. But this is where Cleopatra and her brother differed: she gave careful thought to every action.

Cleopatra saw an opportunity in Caesar, whose large army would ensure her return to the throne. Legend has it that she wrapped herself in an Oriental rug she gave as a gift to the Roman emperor. (This allowed her to meet him without raising any suspicions or getting herself killed.) Sure enough, Caesar fell madly in love with the bewitching Egyptian and promptly returned her to power.

Cleopatra's shrewd marketing skills secured her power, money, and men more than once. When Caesar was assassinated (Rome was predictable in its unpredictability), the new ruler of Rome requested her presence. Not only did she keep him waiting, but when she did arrive, it was on a gilded boat with purple sails, and oars rowing to music. The woman knew how to make an entrance! And her plan paid off—Marc Antony was enchanted.

Cleopatra made one miscalculation, though. She fell as deeply for Antony as he had for her. While most men were intimidated by her intellect, Marc Antony was her admirer and her equal. He won her affection by adding scrolls to her treasured library, where they spent evenings eating extravagant meals and reading together. They were the Romeo and Juliet of their time, and their love story ended just as tragically.

Rome was still embroiled in conflict, with the heir to the empire, Octavian, plotting against Antony and Cleopatra. They engaged in a war they couldn't win, weakening Cleopatra's beloved country. In the midst of the chaos, Antony heard a rumor that Cleopatra had died, and he fell on his own sword rather than live without her. Cleopatra buried her love, settled things with Octavian, put on her best clothing and makeup, and committed suicide. She was buried with Antony, as was the legacy of her family line.

Learn from Cleopatra's legacy: Don't be afraid to show people how smart you are, to use your intellect, to be different from other girls, to be better than the boys. Some people might be intimidated. Some might lash out. But the ones who matter will get you. Just focus on being the best you that you can be.

HISTORY IS WRITTEN BY THE WINNERS

You might be asking yourself why Cleopatra is always portrayed as a conniving seductress. There's a good reason for that: Octavian rewrote history. He wanted to make it clear that he was the rightful ruler, and he thought it looked better if his enemy were a foreigner who used her feminine wiles, rather than his own countryman. But it's important to remember the truth—that Cleopatra was an incredibly intelligent and insightful leader who made her country a better place to live.

JOAN OF ARC

WAR HEROINE AND SAINT

BORN: 1412 · DIED: 1431

- Followed her visions to lead men in battle during the Hundred Years' War
- Executed for witchcraft and dressing like a man
- Canonized by the Roman Catholic Church 500 years after her death

"ONE LIFE IS ALL WE HAVE AND WE LIVE IT AS WE BELIEVE IN LIVING IT. BUT TO SACRIFICE WHAT YOU ARE AND TO LIVE WITHOUT BELIEF, THAT IS A FATE MORE TERRIBLE THAN DYING." —JOAN OF ARC

The Middle Ages weren't easy on anyone— no indoor plumbing, endless layers of uncomfortable clothing, and a society dominated by men trying to kill each other. So when a teenage girl told a French prince that God had assigned her to help him win a war that had been raging for decades, you can bet that he was a little skeptical. But Joan of Arc would lead armies into battle, stand by the king's side at his coronation, and give up her life for a purpose she believed in, all before she turned 20. It took the Catholic Church half a millennium to recognize and appreciate Joan's unwavering faith, but this remarkable young girl is known today as the church's Patron Saint of France.

Joan was born to tenant farmers in the rural French village of Domrémy. For a girl born to a poor family in the 1400s, education wasn't a priority— Joan never learned to read or write. Instead, her father taught her how to tend to the animals, and her mother taught her how to love the Catholic Church. And she did both extremely well.

"I WAS ADMONISHED TO ADOPT FEMININE CLOTHES; I REFUSED, AND STILL REFUSE. AS FOR OTHER AVOCATIONS OF WOMEN, THERE ARE PLENTY OF OTHER WOMEN TO PERFORM THEM." —JOAN OF ARC

By the time she was 13 years old, Joan was devout. So when she began to receive what she believed were messages from God accompanied by a bright light, she didn't question her own sanity. She listened. Over time, the messages became clearer and more specific: St. Michael and St. Catherine told Joan that she would be the savior of France and needed to seek out Charles VII (son of the last French king).

Joan was born into the middle of the Hundred Years' War between England and France, which (as you can tell by the name) had been going on for quite a while. At this point, England was winning, had invaded much of France—including Joan's village—and had claimed sovereignty over the country. But the people of France sensed an

opportunity: King Henry V of England and King Charles VI of France died within months of each other, leaving an opening for Charles VII to reclaim the crown.

Enter: Joan and her divine guidance. In 1428, Joan's visions told her to seek out army commander Robert de Baudricourt in Vaucouleurs and convince him of her mission. He initially rejected the notion, but people rallied behind her, citing a popular prophecy that said a maiden would come to save France. So, the commander gave Joan a horse and sent her to Charles with some soldier escorts.

Joan cut off her long hair and dressed as a man to protect her mission and her virtue on her long journey to the palace. (A woman traveling among soldiers in a dress was likely to be harassed.) Once there, she convinced Charles of her intention to see him crowned king, as ordained by God. Charles may not have believed Joan, but he had nothing to lose by letting her proceed with her quest. He gave the 17-year-old peasant girl a suit of armor and a white horse and sent her into battle.

It's hard to imagine having the kind of unwavering faith Joan showed in following her visions into battle, but it certainly helped her see her quest through. No one could explain how a young girl with no military experience was able to lead French soldiers to victory time after time. She had courage and intellect, but Joan also gave her people what they needed most: hope. As the French forced the English to retreat, Charles cautiously followed in her wake to Reims, where he was crowned King Charles VII of France.

In the end, though, Charles let his bruised ego get the better of him. Joan had been captured in battle, sold to the English, and then handed over to the church, which tried her for crimes of witchcraft, heresy (going against the church), and dressing like a man. (Oddly enough, they were most upset by the cross-dressing, which they deemed a sin against nature.) Charles was still unsure of the divine origins of Joan's mission, but he was certain that this young girl was a more powerful force than he was. He left her to fend for herself to ensure he'd keep the throne she procured for him.

The trials lasted a full year. At first they were public—an attempt to embarrass Charles through his girl soldier. But when Joan was the picture of grace under pressure, often annoying her questioners with clever replies, they began interrogating her in private. She was firm in her belief in God and His plan for her. Unable to prove anything except that she dressed as a man, the tribunal sentenced her to burn at the stake. She was 19 years old.

Although Joan's story doesn't have a happy ending, her legacy of bravery and faith live on in France to this day. Her courage gave the French people the hope and renewed strength they needed to take back their country. Joan died before the war ended, but France owes its victory to her.

JOAN'S REDEMPTION

In 1456, three years after the war's end, Charles held a new trial and declared Joan innocent of all charges. Nearly 500 years later, in 1920, the Roman Catholic Church canonized her—she became the patron saint of France.

POCAHONTAS

AMBASSADOR AND PEACEKEEPER

BORN: 1595 · DIED: 1617

- The favorite daughter of chief Powhatan
- Convinced her father to have mercy on the starving Jamestown settlers
- Converted to Christianity and married Englishman John Rolfe

"[POCAHONTAS WAS] THE INSTRUMENT TO PRESERVE THIS COLONY FROM DEATH, FAMINE, AND UTTER CONFUSION." —JOHN SMITH

Everyone knows the story of Pocahontas, right? Saved a man named John Smith from beheading, fell in love, adopted a pet raccoon. No, wait, that was a cartoon. The real story is much simpler than Disney's captivating tale of bravery, adventure, and romance. Pocahontas claimed her place in history not with courage, but with compassion.

Pocahontas was the favorite daughter of chief Powhatan, who ruled over thousands of people. (The fact that she was prized over his 26 other children hints at how exceptional she was.) When English settlers arrived in Powhatan's territory, cold and starving, their fate fell into the hands of the 12-year-old girl and her powerful

WHAT'S IN A NAME

Every once in a while, a childhood nickname sticks (whether we like it or not). That's what happened to Pocahontas. History has been calling her by her nickname—which means "playful little girl"—for 400 years. Those close to her also called her Matoaka, meaning "bright stream between the hills," but her birth name was Amonute. By the time she died, she had adopted an English name: Rebecca. While we don't know much about Pocahontas, we can guess by her nicknames that she was a bright, happy person.

father. The chief's first thoughts were not welcoming, but Pocahontas convinced him to give the newcomers a chance.

HAVING A GREEN THUMB PAYS OFF

As a Native American girl, Pocahontas would have been taught early on how to plant, harvest, and cook food, how to collect water, and how to tend fires. The English settlers had been relying on food they brought with them, rather than growing their own. That was shortsighted, considering that when their supplies ran out, they had no idea what to do. Without the charity of Pocahontas and her tribe, the settlers would have starved. Lesson learned: it can't hurt to know how to grow a tomato!

You probably know what comes next—the famous scene where young Pocahontas throws herself over John Smith at the moment of his execution. But historians believe that Smith was never in danger. The "execution" was likely a Powhatan ritual to symbolize his death as an Englishman and rebirth as a member of the tribe.

No one clued Smith in, though. In a letter to Queen Anne, he wrote, "... at the minute of my execution, [Pocahontas] hazarded the beating out of her own brains to save mine; and not only that, but so prevailed with her father, that I was safely conducted to Jamestown." After that, Pocahontas routinely visited Jamestown with food for the settlers. Because these first settlers had no idea how to grow their own food, her kindness saved them from starvation.

All went relatively well between the tribe and the settlers until John Smith was injured and returned to England for treatment. Food was harder to come by, due to a drought, and relations between the two groups quickly fell apart. Captain Samuel Argall decided to use the chief's favorite daughter as leverage. He kidnapped her and held her for ransom, but the chief failed to satisfy his demands. Pocahontas was forced to stay among the English.

Almost always content, Pocahontas eventually grew to like being with the settlers—especially one in particular. Widower John Rolfe felt the same way about her. In 1614, Pocahontas converted to Christianity, took the name Rebecca, and married Rolfe. Less than a year later, they welcomed son Thomas Rolfe, and a new era of peace began between the English and the Native Americans.

"IT IS POCAHONTAS TO WHOM MY HEARTY AND BEST THOUGHTS ARE, AND HAVE BEEN A LONG TIME SO ENTANGLED, AND ENTHRALLED IN SO INTRICATE A LABYRINTH THAT I [COULD NOT] UNWIND MYSELF THEREOUT."

—JOHN ROLFE, IN A LETTER CONFESSING HIS LOVE FOR POCAHONTAS

The Virginia Company soon realized that the Rolfe family was exactly the symbol of success they needed to recruit people and money for their settlement. They packed the Rolfes onto a ship bound for London, where they were introduced to King James I and Queen Anne as ambassadors from Jamestown. Pocahontas easily endeared herself to the people of England. Unfortunately, she didn't survive the trip home, and peace between the English and the Native Americans didn't last. Her legacy of kindness, though, has lived on for 400 years.

Truthfully, Pocahontas had to be courageous as often as she was compassionate. New things could prove dangerous—even life-threatening—in her world. For her to welcome new people and places as happily as she did, she needed to be at least a little bit brave. Her easy contentment and fearless compassion saved lives. Pocahontas shows us that you don't have to break records, lead armies, or write bestsellers to make your mark on the world. Being kind can be enough.

ELIZA LUCAS

AGRICULTURALIST AND BUSINESSWOMAN

BORN: 1722 · DIED: 1793

- First person in the United States to cultivate indigo
- Founded the indigo-export business that bolstered South Carolina's economy for decades

"I BEG LEAVE HERE TO ACKNOWLEDGE PARTICULARLY MY OBLIGATION TO YOU FOR . . . MY EDUCATION, WHICH I ESTEEM A MORE VALUEABLE FORTUNE THAN ANY YOU COULD NOW HAVE GIVEN ME." –ELIZA LUCAS IN A LETTER TO HER FATHER

When you've got a lot on your plate, you have two options: mope about it, or rise to the occasion. Most people get around to the rising part after a little moping, and that's fine. But the ones who make history tend to go straight to rising.

17-year-old Eliza Lucas was one of those history-making people. When her father was called to serve the military, she rolled up her sleeves and got to work running his three plantations. But she didn't just oversee the business—she actively involved herself in making it successful.

In the mid-1700s, girls of Eliza's age and social class would typically prepare for marriage. And a girl's education (or, more often, lack thereof) was typically based on the assumption that she would be a wife and mother. Luckily for Eliza, her life was anything but typical. She was born and raised on the Caribbean island of Antigua, and she moved to her grandfather's South Carolina

"HER UNDERSTANDING, AIDED BY AN UNCOMMON STRENGTH OF MEMORY, HAD BEEN SO HIGHLY CULTIVATED AND IMPROVED BY TRAVEL AND EXTENSIVE READING, AND WAS SO RICHLY FURNISHED, AS WELL WITH SCIENTIFIC, AS PRACTICAL KNOWLEDGE, THAT HER TALENT FOR CONVERSATION WAS UNRIVALED, AND HER COMPANY WAS SEDULOUSLY SOUGHT AFTER BY ALL...."

—EXCERPT FROM HER DEATH NOTICE IN THE SOUTH CAROLINA *CITY GAZETTE*

BLUE JEANS

Your favorite wardrobe staple might look a lot different today if not for agriculturalists like Eliza. While indigo has been used for millennia as a dye for all sorts of textiles, its most popular application is in denim. Manufacturers don't use it just for its deep blue hue, though. They also use it because of how it interacts with clothing.

While most dyes become part of the fabric, indigo binds to the outside of the threads. When washed, a little bit of the dye comes off and takes with it a bit of the hard denim fabric. That's why good jeans get softer and more comfortable with every wash. (It's also why you should always wash jeans before you first wear them—otherwise the dye could bleed onto everything you brush up against!) If Eliza hadn't brought indigo to the United States, who knows if jeans would be so popular today?

plantations when she was 14. In between, her father sent her to school in England, where she studied French, music, and her favorite subject: botany.

That interest in agriculture spurred Eliza to spend years testing various crops, looking for one that would flourish in the South Carolina soil and climate. Eliza tried to cultivate ginger, cotton, and alfalfa before settling her hopes on indigo, which she knew the textile industry needed for fabric dye. She also knew that the English would much rather buy it from their own colonies than from their economic rival, the French.

Eliza's father sent her indigo seeds from the plant's natural home in the Caribbean, and she set to work. Between frost and bad luck, the first two years were rough for the indigo crop. Then the French West Indies outlawed exporting indigo seeds so they could maintain control of the crop, and the stakes were higher

than ever. But the third try was the charm, and Eliza's indigo crop produced healthy plants and enough seeds to keep things going.

Now came the hard part: turning plants into dyes. Eliza's father hired a man named Nicholas Cromwell from the West Indies to show her the process. When Nicholas saw how good Eliza's dye was, he suddenly saw her as a threat to his own country's indigo business. He sabotaged the batch. Rather than let the setback stop them, Eliza and her father hired Patrick Cromwell to clean up his brother's mess and ensure a good product.

Making dye from plants was no easy task in the 1700s. First, farmers had to harvest the indigo at exactly the right time to get the deepest color. Then workers (usually slaves) had to cover the cuttings with water and mash them for anywhere from eight to twenty hours. And finally, the dye had to be dried into cakes that could be shipped by boat to other countries.

That was a lot of work to go through once, but now Eliza had to do it twice, and there was still the risk that the dye wouldn't sell. But the English were thrilled with Eliza's product, declaring it even better than French dye. Eliza shared her planting methods with other

farmers in her area, and soon South Carolina was exporting thousands of pounds of indigo per year. By 1775, the state manufactured and exported more than 1 million pounds of dye annually. In today's money, that would be worth 30 million dollars!

Indigo exports sustained the South Carolina economy for 30 years, thanks to one enterprising teenager. Eliza was so admired and respected for her contribution that President George Washington attended her funeral in 1793, honoring her by helping to carry her casket from the church. She was eventually the first woman inducted into the South Carolina Business Hall of Fame.

CREDIT WHERE IT'S DUE

While Eliza managed the business side of the plantation, she wasn't the one tilling the soil. Her family had 20 slaves working the property. Not only did they do the physical work, but they probably used their own knowledge of planting to help Eliza figure out how to get an indigo crop to grow in South Carolina soil. In fact, some of those slaves might have had first-hand knowledge of indigo—the British had brought slavery to the Caribbean and thought nothing of forcing the slaves to move wherever they wanted them to go. All the business and botany know-how in the world couldn't have made Eliza's plantation a success without these hardworking men and women.

PHILLIS WHEATLEY

POET

BORN: 1753 · DIED: 1784

- First black author—male or female—to have a published book of poetry
- Learned English at age 9 and published her first poem at age 14

"THOU DIDST, IN STRAINS OF ELOQUENCE REFIN'D, INFLAME THE SOUL, AND CAPTIVATE THE MIND."

–PHILLIS WHEATLEY, WRITING ABOUT REVEREND GEORGE WHITEFIELD

By her early twenties, Phillis Wheatley was a published poet who could count Founders John Hancock and George Washington among her biggest fans. The admiration her poetry inspired was exceptional for anyone, but especially for a woman in the 1700s. Add that she was black and a slave, and her story sounds like something of a miracle. Then you find out that she couldn't read or speak English until she was nine years old, but she published her first poem at age 14, and you realize that Phillis was something of a miracle.

Before she was Phillis Wheatley, she was a nameless little girl shivering down to her bare feet on a dock in the Boston harbor. She had been kidnapped from her home in Africa and sold into slavery, barely surviving the long journey by ship to the British colonies in America. That's how she came to be the property of Mrs. Susanna Wheatley one August day in 1761.

Susanna's twins, Mary and Nathaniel, were 18 years old and had one foot out the door. Facing the prospect of an empty nest, Susanna was hoping to find a companion in the harbor that day. The group of slaves

SLAVERY IN AMERICA

By 1761, when Phillis arrived in America, the British had been bringing African slaves to the colonies for more than 100 years. And the slave trade wouldn't stop for 100 more. White men and women used men and women of color for everything from planting and harvesting to cooking and cleaning with little concern for them, at best. At worst, slaves were subject to hostility, abuse, and even murder. Phillis had a small hand in helping to bring an end to slavery.

surrounding Phillis were being sold at a discount because they were too old, too young, or too weak for hard labor. When Susanna spotted the delicate 7-year-old girl in the crowd, she knew she had found who she was looking for.

Phillis was named after the boat that took her from Africa and the family who called her their property—generally not a great start. But the Wheatleys were kind people, and they nurtured Phillis's innate curiosity and intellect. In less than two years, Phillis was reading and writing English fluently. From there, she learned Latin, studied the

Bible, and began following in the footsteps of her favorite poets, John Milton and Alexander Pope.

Susanna Wheatley was Phillis's biggest advocate. She recognized the girl's exceptional talent, and she made sure her poems got into the right hands. Thanks to her, a local paper published Phillis's first poem when she was just 14 years old. Phillis's next poem, which she wrote in remembrance of Reverend George Whitefield, was so beautiful, and the Reverend so beloved, that her words reached and affected some of the most influential people in both America and England. Phillis hoped to turn her newfound fame into a publishing deal.

By the time she was 18, Phillis had compiled a few dozen poems that she hoped to turn into a book. Susanna searched for willing publishers all over the colonies but didn't find any takers. Finally, she reached out to Countess of Huntingdon Selina Hastings in London, who had known Reverend Whitefield. The Countess found a publisher who not only was willing to publish the poetry of a young slave girl, but also actually considered her social standing an asset. (When he asked for proof of her

JOHN MILTON

ESSAY ON MAN & Other Poems

authorship, a number of well-known men and women, including John Hancock, were happy to vouch for Phillis.)

Now a published author in England, Phillis traveled there with Nathaniel Wheatley and spent six weeks meeting with dignitaries, philanthropists, and scholars. She then returned home to a pleasant surprise: the Wheatleys decided to grant her legal freedom. Although her owners had been far more gracious and supportive than most, being free meant everything to Phillis.

Phillis continued to write as a free woman. Her poem about George Washington, who had just accepted a post as commander of the Continental Army in 1775, secured her an invitation to meet the man himself in Cambridge, Massachusetts. Phillis believed deeply in Washington's cause, and in his leadership.

In the end, the slave ship's captain was right about Phillis's weak constitution. She died in her early thirties. But she accomplished more in 15 years than most people do in a lifetime. Phillis Wheatley's contributions to both poetry and black history still reverberate today.

THE POWER OF EDUCATION

Phillis was an extraordinary person, but she was also extraordinarily lucky to have the Wheatleys, who educated her and encouraged her to use her gifts. Most slaves were treated more like property than people, with no concern for their thoughts and feelings. It was extremely unusual for a slave to be allowed to learn to read and write, and this opportunity let Phillis' strengths shine.

Receiving an education changed both Phillis's life and the world we live in because her passionate words live on in her poems. But her legacy of literary achievement is also a legacy of change. Abolitionists (people who wanted to end slavery) pointed to people like Phillis when advocating for the rights of men and women kept as slaves. She was an example of a kind and intelligent African American woman whose access to relative freedom allowed her to contribute to society just like everyone else—something slave-owners and many people of the time didn't want to admit.

PHILLIS WHEATLEY

ÉLISABETH VIGÉE-LEBRUN

PORTRAIT ARTIST

BORN: 1755 · DIED: 1842

- Was a sought-after portrait artist by the age of 15
- Developed her own style of painting in a time when both innovation and female painters were frowned upon

"PAINTING AND LIVING HAVE ALWAYS BEEN ONE AND THE SAME THING FOR ME." —ÉLISABETH VIGÉE-LEBRUN

From an early age, Élisabeth Vigée-LeBrun gravitated toward art. She doodled in the margins of her notebooks in school and even occasionally drew on the walls (her teachers were annoyed; Élisabeth was punished). She was only 13 when her father died and she had to apply her talents toward earning an income.

Luckily for her mother and brother, Élisabeth was as skilled as she was passionate. By the age of 15, she was making enough money to support her family. And when her mother remarried a terrible man, she made enough money to support him, too. Her wicked stepfather

wore her father's clothes and took her earnings. So she did the only thing a woman could do in 1776 to escape—she got married.

Élisabeth learned the hard way that desperation makes bad decisions. Like her stepfather, her husband Jean-Baptiste LeBrun took all the money she earned and made none of his own. Even worse than her stepfather, he spent her money on gambling, alcohol, and other women. She was miserable. With no way to physically escape this time, she found her freedom in painting.

Élisabeth came by her artistic talents honestly—her father was a successful portrait painter. But what made her famous was putting her own spin on portraiture. The artistic style of the time was pompous and stuffy, with women in powdered faces, elaborate outfits, and enormous wigs. But Élisabeth preferred a more natural look. Her paintings exhibited beauty with honesty, humility, and warmth.

REBRANDING MARIE ANTOINETTE

Marie Antoinette had an image problem. France was on the brink of revolution, ready to overthrow the royals for being out of touch. They saw the queen's lavish lifestyle as an insult and blamed her for their poverty. Élisabeth painted Marie Antoinette much more softly than others had done. Her portraits made the queen seem more maternal and relatable. Unfortunately, the damage had already been done and the French people were unmoved.

Word got around about Élisabeth's unique talents, and the queen of France herself sought her out. Marie Antoinette invited Élisabeth to be an official court artist, paying her well and helping to solidify her reputation. Élisabeth later wrote in her memoirs, "I was very much in awe of Her Majesty's imposing air; but she spoke to me in such a kindly fashion that her warm sympathy soon dissolved any such impression." (This was a much different take on the queen than the majority of the French people held.)

Thanks to her work for Marie Antoinette, Élisabeth found a constant clientele in the French aristocracy. Queens, princesses, and noblewomen alike wanted to feel beautiful without all the fuss that the late-1700s imposed. But with the French Revolution brewing, Élisabeth found herself being painted, too—by the French public, as one of the elitist airheads on the wrong side of history.

For her own safety, Élisabeth packed up her daughter and fled the country. Exile was kind to her, though. Her reputation for graceful artwork followed her from country to country, and she found plenty of work to support herself. She also took the opportunity to leave her terrible husband behind, writing him a letter from Russia that essentially said she was better off without him.

Élisabeth returned to France in 1802, when more than 250 of her fellow artists petitioned for her to come back. She continued to paint throughout her life, completing more than 900 works, some of which hang in famous museums like the Louvre and the Met.

Had Élisabeth adhered to conventional methods, had she let society tell her who she was and what she should do, the world would have 900 fewer beautiful works of art. She fought for her vision and paved the way not just for female artists but also for anyone who wants to do things his or her own way.

TALENT ISN'T EVERYTHING

Society wasn't ready for someone as talented and independent as Élisabeth Vigée-LeBrun. She had to prove her worth in a field dominated by men who thought they knew better—and they didn't make it easy. They seized her studio and work because she was profiting without a license. Then they claimed that her artwork wasn't admissible for a license (though more likely, her gender wasn't). Finally, Marie Antoinette greased the wheels and Élisabeth was admitted to the Académie Royale de Peinture et de Sculpture.

While Élisabeth made a good living from painting people in high places, she still didn't impress the art world. Her self-portrait was considered shocking and disgraceful because of her slightly wide smile. She had broken the rules by showing a few teeth.

Élisabeth didn't care whether society was ready for her. She had the courage to believe in her own talents and creative vision. While her paintings are lovely, her real legacy is a lesson in following your own compass.

SYBIL LUDINGTON

WAR HEROINE

BORN: 1761 · DIED: 1839

- Rode 40 miles in pouring rain to alert the militia that British soldiers were burning Danbury, Connecticut
- Remembered as "the female Paul Revere," but actually rode longer and harder than he did

> **"THERE IS NO EXTRAVAGANCE IN COMPARING HER RIDE WITH THAT OF PAUL REVERE AND ITS MIDNIGHT MESSAGE. NOR WAS HER ERRAND LESS EFFICIENT THAN HIS."** –WILLIS FLETCHER JOHNSON

Have you ever heard a friend described as "fearless" and wished you could be more like her? A little fear is healthy (it's what keeps us from burning our hands on a hot stove), but we all have courage within us when we need it. And just one night of courage can change everything.

When colonial Americans decided they wanted freedom from British rule, the British didn't go down without a fight. The Revolutionary War lasted more than 8 years. You might be picturing hardened soldiers on both sides, but many of the people who fought for our country were ordinary men who trained once in a while in case of emergency. When they weren't needed, they lived normal lives at home.

When Colonel Henry Ludington received word that British soldiers were setting fire to Danbury, Connecticut, his troops were spread out all over the county for planting season. The colonel needed a messenger he could trust, one who knew where his men lived and how to get there over rough terrain. Only one person fit the bill: his 16-year-old daughter, Sybil.

Sybil rode her horse, Star, through darkness and driving rain to find her father's troops, all while evading the British and at least one criminal who tried to assault her. She shouted at farmhouses: "The British are burning Danbury! Muster at Ludington's at daybreak!" After riding at a breakneck pace for 40 miles, she returned home at sunrise, soaked and exhausted, to find 400 soldiers ready to march. Not bad for a night's work!

Although Colonel Ludington's men couldn't save Danbury from the fire, they did make the British regret setting the flames in the ensuing Battle of Ridgefield. And Sybil received a personal letter of thanks from General George Washington. But the incredible story of 16-year-old patriot Sybil Ludington quickly faded into the background of the Revolutionary War.

Beyond the letter from Washington, Sybil probably didn't receive any recognition

during her lifetime. She married, had a son, and lived a quiet life. The American people rediscovered Sybil decades after her death, when her great-nephew (historian Louis S. Patrick) wrote an article about her ride. It would take several more decades for her to even be mentioned in classrooms.

Instead, you're more likely to hear about American silversmith Paul Revere, whose famous midnight ride was actually part of a planned military strategy. Revere had one mission: alert Samuel Adams and John Hancock (two of America's Founders) that the British were coming to arrest them. And he was just one of three men who were given the mission and sent out on different routes. But American poet Henry Wadsworth Longfellow immortalized the image of a heroic Revere racing through the streets, shouting, "The British are coming!"

"HEROES HAVE MADE POETS, AND POETS HEROES." –GEORGE WASHINGTON

When Sybil is remembered at all, she's often referred to as "the female Paul Revere." But she deserves to be recognized independently for her courageous actions. She may not have been fearless—she was probably scared to death—but she didn't let that stop her. She knew that her father and her country needed her, and she rose to the challenge.

Sybil's story is a reminder that heroism is in our actions, not in our DNA. Today, she's remembered with an annual 50-kilometer run over hilly terrain in Carmel, New York, that symbolizes her rocky ride. The race finishes near a life-size bronze statue that honors her contribution to America's fight for independence.

LET'S COMPARE

While Paul Revere did risk his life, it's clear that Sybil deserves at least the same amount of recognition and respect. All things considered, Sybil's ride was definitely the more impressive of the two.

	PAUL REVERE	SYBIL LUDINGTON
AGE	41 years old	16 years old
MILITARY BACKGROUND	Member of militia	None
DISTANCE OF RIDE	22-mile planned ride	40-mile unplanned ride
PEOPLE ALERTED	2	Hundreds
WEATHER DURING RIDE	Clear skies	Driving rain
RIDING ATTIRE	Wore pants	Wore a dress

JANE AUSTEN

AUTHOR AND PIONEER OF THE ROMANTIC COMEDY

BORN: 1775 · DIED: 1817

- Barely made a living from her work despite being one of the most famous authors in history
- Insightful human commentary makes her novels as popular and relatable today as ever
- A clear example of someone who followed her passion and wrote what she knew

"INDULGE YOUR IMAGINATION IN EVERY POSSIBLE FLIGHT." –JANE AUSTEN

You know when you get into an argument and think of the perfect thing to say three hours later? Jane Austen didn't have that problem. Known for her razor-sharp wit, she served up snarky pointed comments the way other English women served cups of tea—politely and for the enjoyment of others. Her clever and insightful social commentary was meant to entertain (herself as much as her readers, perhaps), not harm.

Jane was born to write. She was able to "find the funny" in everyday situations and to turn normal people—with all their quirks and flaws—into beloved characters.

And in doing so, she paved the way for the romantic comedies we know and love today. Some of these, like *Bridget Jones' Diary* and *Clueless*, are actually modern-day versions her books (*Pride and Prejudice* and *Emma*, respectively). Her work has even been adapted into action/adventure books and movies (*Pride and Prejudice and Zombies*, *Sense and Sensibility and Sea Monsters*).

But her stories were never about good versus evil (whereas zombies are a pretty clear antagonist). They were about how life and society sometimes get in the way of what people want. And more often than not, they were about people getting in their own way: Mr. Darcy is too proud to allow himself to love Elizabeth, who is silly and poor and not at all whom he should marry. And Elizabeth assumes Mr. Darcy is an irritating snob (which is not untrue), so it takes an entire novel for them to realize they're perfect for each other. Meanwhile, the reader devours every page of simple misunderstandings and biting banter. Not many authors have that kind of pull, and even fewer of them were women in the prim and proper early 1800s.

SPOILER ALERT

Jane made sure that all of her heroines got their happy endings, possibly because she never had one herself. Her one great love—Tom LeFroy—was forced by family to marry for money, and she remained single her whole life.

Thanks to her father, who encouraged education and creativity in his daughters, she was eventually able to earn a living through her writing and to support her mother and sister. But she died long before anyone could know the real impact of her work.

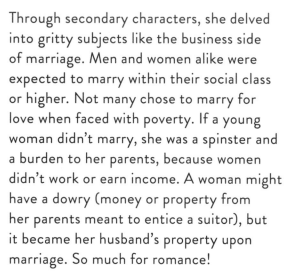

Like many great minds, Jane was ahead of her time. When society dictated how women should think, act, speak, and marry, she created characters who did things their own way. But she didn't gloss over the hardships suffered at the hands of an unforgiving social structure.

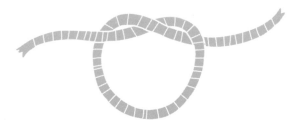

Through secondary characters, she delved into gritty subjects like the business side of marriage. Men and women alike were expected to marry within their social class or higher. Not many chose to marry for love when faced with poverty. If a young woman didn't marry, she was a spinster and a burden to her parents, because women didn't work or earn income. A woman might have a dowry (money or property from her parents meant to entice a suitor), but it became her husband's property upon marriage. So much for romance!

Jane also showed how property law affected families at the time. Property could only be passed down from man to man. In the case of the Bennets in *Pride and Prejudice*, this meant they would be tossed out on their ears upon Mr. Bennet's death if Elizabeth

"WE ALL HAVE OUR BEST GUIDES WITHIN US, IF ONLY WE WOULD LISTEN." –FANNY PRICE IN *MANSFIELD PARK*

didn't fancy marrying her weasely cousin, Mr. Collins (which she didn't). While Jane's heroines never suffered such a fate, she made it clear that other women had—and how she felt about the practice. She gave a human face to the inhumane practices of her time, and gave us a deeper understanding than any history book ever could.

Readers today still can't get enough of Jane Austen. Clubs have formed to celebrate her. Whole books have been written on her witticisms alone. She gave us stories that are as relatable as they are epic, strong female characters to lead us by example, and an entire genre of binge-worthy books and movies. And if all that's not enough, she also gave us the inspiration to follow our passion. She did, and the world is better for it.

WRITE WHAT YOU KNOW

"Write what you know." You may have heard that age-old piece of advice before. Whether you're completing an assignment or, like Jane Austen, you're just drawn to storytelling, it's good advice. It certainly worked out for Jane. She knew people—she knew how they felt, what made them tick. She knew what society wanted for them, and what they wanted for themselves. Her witty exploration of how those two things didn't always line up is what makes her books relatable to this day, 200 hundred years later. So the next time you're stumped, start with what you know and go from there.

SACAGAWEA

EXPLORER AND INTERPRETER

BORN: 1789 · DIED: 1812

- Joined the Lewis and Clark expedition as a guide and interpreter at 15 years old
- Taught the men how to forage for edible and medicinal plants
- Kept her calm and saved irreplaceable documents when her boat nearly capsized
- Represented the interests of the U.S. government to Native American tribes

"YOUR WOMAN, SACAGAWEA, DESERVED A GREATER REWARD THAN WE HAD IT IN OUR POWER TO GIVE." —WILLIAM CLARK IN A LETTER TO CHARBONNEAU

Now that you can Google the answer to any question, it's hard to imagine a time when plants, animals, and places were completely unknown to us. Explorers like the famous Lewis and Clark are why Google has those answers—they traveled thousands of miles, cataloguing every creature and crevice they came across. But without a 15-year-old Native American girl named Sacagawea, their greatest mission would have been impossible.

Our country looked very different in 1803, when President Thomas Jefferson asked Meriwether Lewis and William Clark to explore America's newly purchased land (known as the Louisiana territory, it included 15 of today's states). Lewis and Clark called the expedition, "The Corps of Discovery," and their mission was to learn and relay as much information as possible about the territory and the Native Americans who already called it home. In need of guidance, the Corps enlisted the help of French fur trader Toussaint Charbonneau and his young Native American bride, Sacagawea.

Sacagawea had a difficult life. Kidnapped by the Hidatsa tribe (a rival of her own Shoshone tribe) at the age of 12, she was taken hundreds of miles from home and was gambled away to Charbonneau, who took her as his second wife. When Lewis and Clark came to the Hidatsa-Mandan villages in search of translators, Sacagawea was just 15 years old and already six months pregnant with Charbonneau's son, Jean-Baptiste. And the two explorers certainly weren't going to make things easier for her.

While dragging a young mother on a journey for thousands of miles might seem a little strange, Sacagawea was the perfect woman for the job. Lewis and Clark knew her presence (as a Native American, a woman, and a mother) would signal to tribes that the expedition was peaceful. Because food and health aren't guaranteed during an expedition like this, her knowledge of the land and of which plants could be eaten or used to make medicine would also come in handy. But it was her Shoshone language skills that made her essential to the mission.

The Corps traveled the first leg of their journey by boat, but carrying their supplies through the Rocky Mountains required horses. And who had horses to spare? Sacagawea's own Shoshone tribe. Lewis and Clark had carefully planned for this negotiation, but they could never have

THE DANGERS OF DISCOVERY

Traveling thousands of miles through the unknown is bound to be a little dangerous, but the Lewis and Clark expedition turned almost deadly on a regular basis. The explorers had to escape run-ins with buffalo and bears, survive freezing temperatures, and stave off starvation when food was scarce. And in 1804, a time when most of modern medicine had yet to be invented, a simple fever could be fatal. In fact, it *was* fatal for Sergeant Charles Floyd, who died three months into the trip. Sacagawea herself nearly died from a similar illness. Clark almost drowned in a flash flood. Lewis literally dodged a bullet in a hunting mishap and once nearly fell off a cliff. Luckily for the Corps of Discovery, Sergeant Floyd was the only member who didn't make it home safe and sound.

anticipated their good fortune in choosing Sacagawea for the task. When introduced to the Shoshone chief, Cameahwait, she immediately recognized him as the brother she'd been taken away from years earlier. Their cheerful reunion led to Cameahwait's offering extra supplies and instructions for safe passage in addition to the horses.

Despite rediscovering the home that the Hidatsu had torn her away from, Sacagawea was happy to continue on with the expedition. Lewis mentioned this in his journal: "Sacagawea shows no emotion or joy at being again in her native land. If she has enough to eat and a few trinkets to wear, we believe she would be contented anywhere." Which is to say, Sacagawea rolled with the punches.

But she also spoke up when she wanted something. As the explorers drew closer to the Pacific Ocean, they got word of a beached whale. To the men in the expedition, this meant food and oil. To Sacagawea, this meant seeing not only the ocean for the first time, but also one of its greatest creatures. So when Lewis and Clark told her to stay at camp, she made it clear to them that she *deserved* to see the ocean.

ODD WOMAN OUT

Have you ever felt like the odd person out? Sacagawea knew the feeling. She was the only woman in an expedition of 33 men (34, if you count her infant son—and she had to carry him on her back for thousands of miles). But Sacagawea didn't let that scare her. She repeatedly proved to those men that she was an important member of the team.

When meat was scarce and the men were starving, Sacagawea taught them how to find plants, roots, berries, and even tree bark to eat. When they encountered Native Americans, she acted as peacekeeper and interpreter. And when her own husband let his fear of water get the better of him and nearly capsized their small boat, she stayed calm under pressure and recovered irreplaceable documents from the water. Sacagawea's resilience was her greatest asset.

Sacagawea's ability to make the best of any situation routinely saved the Corps of Discovery from disaster, and Lewis and Clark were immensely grateful for her company on their long journey. In a letter to Toussaint Charbonneau, Clark wrote, "Your woman, Sacagawea, deserved a greater reward than we had it in our power to give." Although Sacagawea didn't see a reward in her lifetime, she is a legendary figure in American history. You can find her face on the dollar coin, and her spirit of resilience in women throughout the country.

MARY SHELLEY

AUTHOR AND INVENTOR OF SCIENCE FICTION

BORN: 1797 · DIED: 1851

- Born to progressive parents who taught her to think for herself
- Published her first novel (the first-ever science fiction novel), *Frankenstein*, at 19
- Her second novel, *The Last Man*, was the first post-apocalyptic tale

"NOTHING CONTRIBUTES SO MUCH TO TRANQUILIZE THE MIND AS A STEADY PURPOSE." —MARY SHELLEY

When you're having a bad day (or a bad week), what do you reach for? Maybe you grab a set of colored pencils to color your way to calm. Or a game controller that will let you zone out for hours while you level up. What about a pen, so you can capture those swirling thoughts of annoyance on paper? Mary Shelley took the pen-and-paper route when life got on her nerves—a habit that would lead her to create one of the most famous monsters in literary history when she was just 19 years old.

Mary's life started out happily enough, with parents who were smart and progressive in a time when women weren't given much credit. Her father, William Godwin, was a philosopher and political writer who showered his daughter with books and clever friends to discuss them with. Her mother, Mary Wollstonecraft, was a writer, philosopher,

FRANKENSTEIN AT A GLANCE

Frankenstein; or The Modern Prometheus is a story of an arrogant young scientist who becomes obsessed with defeating death. His plans go horribly wrong when he tries to bring a man back to life and accidentally creates an unstoppable monster instead.

and women's rights advocate who is considered by historians to be one of the founders of feminism.

Sadly, Mary's mother died just days after giving birth to her. Her father eventually remarried, to a woman named Mary Jane Clairmont, and Mary's childhood began to resemble a fairytale—Cinderella. Despite Mary's love of learning, her wicked stepmother decided she wasn't worth a formal education. So Mary stayed home while Clairmont's own daughter was sent away to school.

Mary may have gotten the better deal, though. Between her father's extensive library and visits from his famously intellectual friends, she received more of a broad and insightful education than any girl her age. And although Mary's mother wasn't alive to pass along her feminist ideals, Mary inherited her intelligence and persistence.

SUMMER IN SCOTLAND

Mary spent the summer of 1812 in Scotland with William Baxter (a friend of her father's) and his family. Surrounded by the beauty of nature and with the companionship of Baxter's daughters, she had her first taste of a normal, happy life. While she enjoyed her time there, she knew it would never inspire the kind of tales she loved to write. The introduction to *Frankenstein* included these lines: "I wrote then—but in a most common-place style. It was beneath the trees of the grounds belonging to our house, or on the bleak sides of the woodless mountains near, that my true compositions, the airy flights of my imagination, were born and fostered." Mary understood that happiness and creativity didn't always go hand in hand.

Mary also inherited her parents' open-minded views about romance. At age 16, she fell madly in love with a married man. Percy Bysshe Shelley was 21 years old, an established writer and poet, and a student of William Godwin. But that didn't stop him from leaving his pregnant wife in England to run away with young Mary to Europe. From the moment they met until Percy drowned in a shipwreck eight years later, their relationship was plagued by drama, infidelity, and the death of loved ones.

While everything in Mary's life to this point was unusual (to say the least), the inspiration for her most famous creation was fairly ordinary: a group of friends sitting around a wood-burning fire, talking. Sure, the subject matter turned a little grim. But such were the times and the company she kept. On one such dark and stormy night in Switzerland, Lord Byron (a famous Romantic poet himself) challenged his friends to each write their own ghost story.

Mary struggled against writer's block, dreading each morning when the others would ask whether she had thought of a story. This simple exercise between friends suddenly felt like a test she might fail. Finally, a late-night conversation about life and death sparked an idea, and Mary penned the first lines of a short story about a man brought back to life. With Percy's encouragement, she expanded that story into the incredible tale of Frankenstein's monster we know today.

Mary was just 19 years old when she wrote *Frankenstein.* She published it anonymously at first to avoid sexist backlash against a woman writing such a dark and thrilling novel.

"BEWARE; FOR I AM FEARLESS, AND THEREFORE POWERFUL."

–*FRANKENSTEIN; OR, THE MODERN PROMETHEUS*

(J. K. Rowling used her initials to publish Harry Potter for the same reason nearly two centuries later!) She finally took credit for her masterpiece four years later, in 1822.

Mary Shelley's life was full of the kind of loss, frustration, and conflict that she wouldn't have wished on anyone else. But she was first to admit that without those moments of anger and sadness, she might never have created the monster that has captured our imaginations for 200 years. She used her passion for writing not to find light in the darkness, but to create it.

AHEAD OF HER TIME

Mary Shelley is credited as the inventor of science fiction, which is a pretty big accomplishment all on its own. That means that, without her, books like *A Wrinkle in Time* and *The Time Machine* might never have existed. But Mary didn't stop there. In writing *The Last Man*, she also invented post-apocalyptic fiction—think *The Hunger Games* and *Divergent.* So don't be afraid to think outside the box and try things no one has ever tried. If Mary Shelley never had, your favorite books might not have been written.

ANITA GARIBALDI

REVOLUTIONARY

BORN: 1821 · DIED: 1849

- Taught husband Giuseppe Garibaldi how to ride horses in battle
- Fought side by side with her husband in battle, even while pregnant

"DO NOT BE AFRAID TO LIVE TO CHASE DREAMS. BE AFRAID TO STAND STILL." –ANITA GARIBALDI

Anita Garibaldi's humble beginnings in Brazil were no indication of the strength and passion that would forge her place in history. As a woman born in the 1800s, Anita wasn't raised to expect much from her life. Her family was poor, her surroundings bleak, and her future looked like more of the same—especially when she was forced to marry Manuel Duarte Aguiar at the age of 14. But fate had more in store for Anita than she could imagine.

Italian revolutionary Giuseppe Garibaldi met Ana Maria "Anita" de Jesus Ribeiro da Silva not long after her husband abandoned her to join the Imperial Army. It was love at first sight. Legend has it that Giuseppe was so awestruck by Anita, he could only whisper, "You must be mine." Clearly, she felt the same way, because she joined him on his ship, the *Rio Pardo*, in 1839. They weren't together a month before she was fighting beside him in the battles of Imbituba and Laguna.

NOT HORSING AROUND

Long before the invention of tanks and Humvees, knowing how to ride a horse well could mean the difference between life and death in battle. Anita had grown up around the rough and tumble gaucho culture, and she was a skilled horsewoman. By teaching Giuseppe how to handle horses like a gaucho, she gave her love his best chance at surviving what would be a career of fighting for democracy and freedom.

Anita was no slouch on the battlefield. A fellow fighter described her as "an amalgam of two elemental forces...the strength and courage of a man and the charm and tenderness of a woman, manifested by the daring and vigor with which she had brandished her sword and the beautiful oval of her face that trimmed the softness of her extraordinary eyes." (No wonder Giuseppe was enchanted!)

Anita was pregnant with their first child, Menotti, when she followed Giuseppe into the Battle of Curitibanos. In the midst of the fight, Anita was captured by the enemy and was told Giuseppe was dead. Her captors

didn't realize the power of hope. She wouldn't believe it until she saw his body with her own eyes, so she asked to search the battlefield for him. When Anita failed to find Giuseppe's body, she allowed herself to believe her love might still be alive. She snuck back into the camp, quickly mounted one of the horses there, and took off.

The soldiers chased after her, but Anita was a force to be reckoned with on horseback. The only way they could catch her was to shoot her horse out from under her. Despite a fall so hard it injured her unborn baby, Anita kept running. She waded into the river Canoas, where the soldiers left her for dead. Her incredible strength and her love for Giuseppe helped her survive several days in enemy territory without food or water until she could make her way back to him.

Over the next six years, Anita and Giuseppe married and had four children. (Menotti was born with a skull deformity because of Anita's fall, but he still went on to become a freedom fighter like his father.) While pregnant with their fifth child, Anita accompanied her husband to Italy for another fight, this time against the Austrian Empire. But Anita wouldn't make it home. She and her unborn child died from malaria in Giuseppe's arms.

"THE SOLDIERS CHASED AFTER HER, BUT ANITA WAS A FORCE TO BE RECKONED WITH ON HORSEBACK."

Anita is considered a heroine in her home country for having spent so much of her short life fighting for its freedom. Her actions made history, but her strength and courage make her an inspiration to this day. She lived her life to the fullest, bravely following her passion and fighting for what she believed in. In her lifetime, that meant fighting for freedom. In ours, it can mean standing up against bullies, helping the environment, or fighting for social causes we care about.

THE WOMEN BEHIND THE MEN

Giuseppe Garibaldi has been called a hero, a founding father of Italy, and one of the greatest generals in modern times. But without Anita, his legacy might look very different. Their powerful dynamic isn't uncommon—couples have helped each other and pushed each other to be better throughout history. Cleopatra helped Caesar return to power. Coretta Scott King stood by Martin Luther King, Jr.'s side every step of the way as he worked for equality, and she continued to deliver his message long after he died. When President Franklin Roosevelt was stricken with polio, his wife, Eleanor, helped him govern. These women were partners in achievement, not just footnotes in history. Too many others live in their husbands' shadows, afraid to advocate for themselves. If you have the choice between being quiet and being Cleopatra, be Cleopatra.

MARGARET KNIGHT

INVENTOR

BORN: 1838 · DIED: 1914

- Invented a safety mechanism used in cotton mills all over the country when she was 12
- Invented the flat-bottomed paper bag we still use today
- Sued a man who tried to steal her invention, and won

"I'M ONLY SORRY I COULDN'T HAVE HAD AS GOOD A CHANCE AS A BOY, AND HAVE BEEN PUT TO MY TRADE REGULARLY." —MARGARET KNIGHT

Are you a big fan of the do-it-yourself movement? Between Pinterest and the popularity of home makeover shows, women have access to a lot of DIY inspiration these days. But in the Victorian era of the mid to late 1800s, no one would have guessed that women would someday be rolling up their sleeves just for fun.

Margaret (Mattie) Knight knew from an early age that she was different from other girls. She preferred tools to pretty porcelain dolls. She liked to know how things worked and to get her hands dirty. Mattie paid no attention to the girls who puzzled over the tomboy in their town.

Instead, she spent her time making things, like toys for her brothers and a foot warmer for her mother.

But Mattie had to grow up more quickly than other girls. Without her father, who died when she was young, she and her brothers needed to work to help support the family. Mattie took a job at a textile mill, where she and other children used large machines to make fabric. If one of those machines malfunctioned, the consequences could be deadly.

One day, Mattie heard a machine begin to glitch, but there was nothing anyone could do. The needle flew off the loom and into her coworker's leg. At only 12 years old, Mattie knew that there had to be a safer way to work. So she invented it: a safety mechanism so brilliant that it became standard at cotton mills around the country. Of course, Mattie had yet to realize that she could make a living from her ideas.

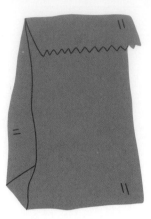

She wouldn't make that mistake with her next big invention. She was working at the Columbia Paper Bag Company when it occurred to her: why not make paper bags with flat bottoms? They would be sturdier than the flimsy paper envelopes people used at the time to carry groceries, and they would certainly hold more. But creating them meant creating a machine that could fold and glue them. Mattie got to work doing exactly that in 1870.

Mattie first created a wooden model of her invention that, although rickety, churned out more than a thousand bags. Now that she was sure of her design, she took the model to a shop where they could build a metal version. The machine worked beautifully, so she quickly went to file a patent (a claim of ownership) on her invention. But someone had beaten her to it.

A sneaky and unscrupulous man named Charles Annan had seen her design in the metal shop, copied it, and filed for a patent on it in his own name. But Mattie had worked too hard to let this one go. She gathered up all of her money and hired a lawyer to sue the man. He tried to argue that his machine

TAKING THINGS FOR GRANTED

It's hard to imagine life without the brown paper bag we know and use today. Or the reusable tote bags fashioned after it. You might think, *Someone had to invent that? Wasn't it just always there?* But that's the point. Without smart people like Mattie thinking about how to make life better and easier, we wouldn't have any of things we take for granted today.

Think about how many different inventions led to the smartphone. We went from the original wired telephones to cordless phones, car phones, and mobile phones, then added in the ability to text, then to access the Internet, and then all the individual apps. And that doesn't account for the software system and physical wiring and hardware. Kind of overwhelming, isn't it? That's why we need as many smart, creative people as we can get!

had key differences, but those differences were clearly just areas where he couldn't remember Mattie's exact design. Between numerous witnesses and journals full of sketches, she easily won her case.

Mattie spent the rest of her life inventing new things, though none of her creations were as impactful as the flat-bottomed bag. But that design was more than enough to secure her place in history. As one of the first women to ever hold a patent, she paved the way for future female inventors. She helped normalize the idea that women could be smart, creative, and handy with mechanics. And, of course, millions of people all over the world still use her invention, almost 150 years later.

MORE ABOUT MATTIE

Margaret Knight was inducted into the National Inventors Hall of Fame in 2006 for her flat-bottomed bag. But in her lifetime, she created 90 or so inventions and patented at least 25 of them. They ranged from shoe-sole cutters to dress protectors. In 1913, *The New York Times* wrote that she, "at the age of seventy, is working twenty hours a day on her 89th invention." She died a year later. Today, more than 7,000 machines produce flat-bottomed paper bags. Mattie's original machine sits in the Smithsonian Museum in Washington, D.C.

"I SIGHED SOMETIMES BECAUSE I WAS NOT LIKE OTHER GIRLS; BUT WISELY CONCLUDED THAT I COULDN'T HELP IT, AND SOUGHT FURTHER CONSOLATION FROM MY TOOLS." —MARGARET KNIGHT

ANNA ELIZABETH DICKINSON

LECTURER AND ACTIVIST

BORN: 1842 · DIED: 1932

- First started advocating publicly for human rights at age 13
- Started her public speaking career unintentionally at age 17
- Addressed Congress and President Lincoln during the Civil War

> "SHE TALKS FAST, USES NO NOTES WHATEVER, NEVER HESITATES FOR A WORD, ALWAYS GETS THE RIGHT WORD IN THE RIGHT PLACE, AND HAS THE MOST PERFECT CONFIDENCE IN HERSELF."

—MARK TWAIN, REFERRING TO ANNA ELIZABETH DICKINSON

Are you the kind of person who tries out for the lead in every play? When the teacher asks for a volunteer, does your hand fly into the air? Some people are born performers—they love an audience, and the audience loves them back. Anna Elizabeth Dickinson was that kind of person. She was smart, charismatic, and charming, and she excited audiences across the country. But she wasn't an actress. She was an activist.

Anna was born into a very different America than we know today. The country was on the brink of the Civil War. Half of the population felt that owning slaves was a right, and the other half (called abolitionists) felt that slavery was immoral. Meanwhile, most of the

THE LIBERATOR.

country agreed that women were inferior to men, belonged in the home, and shouldn't express strong opinions in public. Anna disagreed—wholeheartedly.

A COUNTRY DIVIDED

The Civil War saw America split in two, with northern states (the Union) fighting against southern states (the Confederacy) over the right to keep slaves. After four years of war, the Union won and slavery was abolished. But over 600 thousand soldiers died and much of the South was destroyed.

Today, 150 years later, people still seem to be arguing over America's national identity. That's OK. As long as people have beliefs, they'll have disagreements. The goal is to be able to disagree respectfully, and to work together so that bad moments in history never repeat themselves.

Although Anna was passionate by nature, having parents who encouraged education and activism certainly helped. Her parents were ardent abolitionists who often opened their home to escaped slaves as part of the Underground Railroad (a system

of safe places and passages slaves could use to escape to freedom in the North). Well-known activists and abolitionists like Frederick Douglass and Robert Purvis were friends of the family. In light of all that, Anna's career as an outspoken advocate of human rights isn't much of a surprise.

Anna's career began in writing before flourishing on stage. When she was 13 years old, Anna read an article about a Kentucky teacher who was tarred and feathered (yes, that was a real thing) for writing a letter that opposed slavery. In a fit of shock and anger, Anna wrote a letter to the editor of an abolitionist newspaper, *The Liberator*. The article, which argued that slavery was unconstitutional, was so articulate and analytical that no one would have guessed such a young girl had written it.

Passionately responding to bigotry and sexism became a habit she couldn't help. At age 17, she attended a public debate called "Women's Rights and Wrongs" with the intention of quietly observing. When the lecturer said that women would never work as doctors or lawyers (or in any man's profession), Anna saw red. She stood up and launched into such a fiery speech against him that he actually left the hall!

Though unofficial, Anna's first attempt at public speaking was so exhilarating that she knew she had found her calling. She spoke up at a few more meetings and started to gain a reputation for her smart and passionate speeches. Soon, activists and leaders were inviting her to speak at events and rallies, and her career as a speaker took off.

Anna was considered a welcome breath of fresh air in comparison with the stodgy old men who usually took the stage. She not only enchanted the audience but also held her own against political minds and public opinion alike. She toured the nation on behalf of abolition and women's rights, earning more than enough money to support herself and her four siblings. And at the height of her career, she was invited to address Congress and President Abraham Lincoln.

When Anna's father died during her childhood, she knew that she would someday have to work to support herself. But she never could have imagined the career that would make her the most famous lecturer of her time. She simply followed her passion and her conscience one step at a time. By speaking out for the causes she believed in, she helped the country rally behind them. The establishment of women's rights would take some time, but Anna saw slavery abolished.

If you believe passionately in a cause, get involved. Maybe it's not politics, but animal welfare, environmental issues, or education. Volunteer with organizations that champion your cause. Write letters to your representatives and to newspaper editors. Make people aware of what's going on around them. Find like-minded people who can help you grow, but also seek out and learn from people whose opinions are different from your own. You never know— maybe you can make a career out of making a difference, just like Anna did.

GLOSSOPHOBIA

If you're not a fan of giving speeches, don't worry. You're not alone. In fact, the vast majority of people suffer from glossophobia, which is the technical term for a fear of public speaking. The next time you're freaking out over giving a presentation, you can take comfort in knowing that almost everyone else is freaking out, too. It might also help to know that speaking in public gets easier the more you do it.

ELIZABETH COCHRAN, A.K.A. NELLIE BLY

INVESTIGATIVE JOURNALIST

BORN: 1864 · DIED: 1922

- Began her career in journalism at 18
- Wrote on subjects generally considered too gritty for women
- Spent 10 days in a mental institution to expose how badly the mentally ill were treated
- Traveled around the world in just over 72 days, beating the fictional record in Jules Verne's *Around the World in Eighty Days*

"I ALWAYS HAVE A COMFORTABLE FEELING THAT NOTHING IS IMPOSSIBLE IF ONE APPLIES A CERTAIN AMOUNT OF ENERGY IN THE RIGHT DIRECTION."

—NELLIE BLY

Few things are more frustrating than being told you shouldn't do something just because you're a girl. So when Elizabeth Cochran read an article in the *Pittsburgh Dispatch* calling women who worked outside the home "a monstrosity," she wasn't about to sit there and take it. She wrote a letter to the editor that put the paper in its place and kicked off her career as a successful journalist.

Erasmus Wilson, writing as Quiet Observer (or Q.O.), had titled his article "What Girls Are Good For." Spoiler alert: not much, according to him. He argued that a woman's place was in the home, tending to her husband and children. But Elizabeth had learned early on that life wasn't as black and white as Wilson believed. She had watched her own mother struggle to support their family after her father died, and she knew that many women didn't have the option of staying home. And many more (like her) simply didn't want to.

In her response, 18-year-old Elizabeth wrote that women should be given the same opportunities as men: "Let a youth start as errand boy and he will work his way up until he is one of the firm. Girls are just as smart, a great deal quicker to learn; why, then, can they not do the same?" Managing editor George Madden was so impressed with Elizabeth's passionate writing that he offered her a reporting job and her now-famous pen name, Nellie Bly.

STAND UP

The best way to create change is to stand up for what you believe in, just like Nellie did. In her letter to the *Dispatch*, Nellie called attention to the issue of equal pay, which is something we still struggle with today. Women earn only 79 cents for every dollar that men earn. While things have gotten better since Nellie wrote to the paper, they have a long way to go.

So how do you stay hopeful when change happens so slowly? Take things one step at a time. As Nellie liked to say, "Energy rightly applied and directed will accomplish anything." In other words, you can do anything you put your mind to.

Female reporters weren't uncommon in the 1800s, but they were paid less than men and typically given more "feminine" assignments—on fashion, social events, and gardening. (Nellie received $5 per week—about $112 in today's money and half of what male reporters were paid when starting out.) While Nellie gladly tackled tough subjects like gender inequality and inhumane working conditions, her paper continued to push her toward "women's work." After a year of this, Nellie had had enough. She left Pittsburgh in 1887 with just a note for the sexist writer who started it all: "Dear Q.O., I'm off to New York. Look out for me. Bly."

Nellie had gotten off to a great start as a journalist, but she was still relatively unknown and inexperienced. She would need to do something extraordinary to prove herself in a city known for its newspapers. So, in fearless Nellie Bly fashion, she agreed to have herself committed to the notorious mental institution Blackwell's Island for 10 days so she could get the inside scoop on its operations.

Over the course of several articles with titles like "Behind Asylum Bars," she exposed the terrible treatment of patients, many of whom weren't sick. Some were simply immigrants who spoke little English, others were victims of bigotry (at the time, an emotional woman could be

accused of suffering from "hysteria"). All of the patients there endured meals of rotten food, ice-cold baths, and physical abuse.

The exposé launched Nellie's career as an investigative journalist (one of the first in history), and authorities launched an investigation into New York City's mental health practices. Facilities were given additional funding, extra staff, more supervision, and a number of new regulations. In short, 23-year-old Nellie Bly changed how the mentally ill were treated in America.

Nellie continued to expose mistreatment and misconduct throughout her career as a journalist. By writing about poverty, corruption, mental health, and sexism, she became a voice for people who had been silenced by hardship and an unforgiving society—people like her mother. She paved the way for future journalists and for anyone who sees injustice and stands up to it.

AN INCREDIBLE STUNT

How does a writer top a life-changing exposé? By traveling around the world in just over 72 days, setting a real-world record that beat out the famous fictional one in Jules Verne's *Around the World in Eighty Days*. (This was no small feat in 1889, 15 years before the first commercial plane would hit the runway.) In a stunt devised by Nellie's paper to increase sales, she traveled by ship, horse, rickshaw, train, and even donkey, with just the dress on her back and a small suitcase full of underwear.

MARY PICKFORD

MOVIE STAR AND DIRECTOR

BORN: 1892 · DIED: 1979

- Started a career of acting in, producing, and directing hit films when she was 17
- Became the highest paid actress in history for her time

"YOU MAY HAVE A FRESH START ANY MOMENT YOU CHOOSE, FOR THIS THING THAT WE CALL 'FAILURE' IS NOT THE FALLING DOWN, BUT THE STAYING DOWN." —MARY PICKFORD

We know many actors by name these days, whether because of their work or because of their behavior outside of work. With the click of an app, we can see the personal history of everyone who ever worked on a movie. And if that's not enough, we have magazines and nightly entertainment news programs.

But it wasn't always that easy. In the first years of film, actors and celebrities were two separate things. That long list of credits you see at the end of a movie (and sit through because someone told you there's an after-credits scene)? The enormous salaries that movie stars receive? The very notion of a movie star? That's all because of an impressive young woman named Mary Pickford.

Mary's father died when she was young, and her mother discovered that child stage actors could provide a pretty decent income. By the age of 15, Mary had been acting in plays for nearly a decade. Her stage career ended with a successful two-year run on Broadway, after which she decided to investigate a new medium: moving pictures.

Director D. W. Griffith signed Mary to Biograph Company for $10 a day (nearly $250 in today's money). Years later, Griffith would say, "The thing that most attracted me the day I first saw [Mary] was the intelligence that shone in her face. I found she was thirsty for work and information. She could not be driven from the studio while work was going on. She was—and is—a sponge for experience." That strong work ethic helped her star in 40 films her first year. It also helped movies evolve into the entertainment industry we know and love today.

A LOT HAS CHANGED

Movies were much shorter in Mary's day. They were also completely silent. Have you ever tried watching a movie with the volume muted—no captions? You might be able to get the gist, but you'll probably have a hard time picking up on all the little things that make a movie great. Silent movie stars like Mary had their work cut out for them.

To ensure their audience could understand what was going on, they used exaggerated gestures and facial expressions. Live music played on pianos in individual theaters helped communicate the mood of the scenes (as music does today, only as part of the film). Eventually, studios inserted title cards between scenes, each with a bit of written dialogue or explanation on them. Compared with today's films, silent movies look pretty ridiculous. But they also give us a fresh perspective on how far technology has brought the industry.

Before Mary, movies didn't credit their actors. This might have been so that actors wouldn't have the clout to demand more money, or simply because the medium was so new and still finding its footing. But moviegoers adored Mary, and she soon went from being "the girl with the curls" to the top-billed actress in the business. Her name on a theater marquee sold tickets.

While many actors—even today—focus on the craft or the fame, Mary understood that movies made big money. When her salary at Biograph grew stale, she took a higher-paying contract with another studio. And another after that, and another after that, until she became the highest paid actress in history. She was 22 years old.

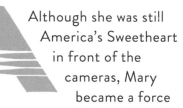 Although she was still America's Sweetheart in front of the cameras, Mary became a force to be reckoned with behind them. At the age of 27, she got together with her future husband Douglas Fairbanks, her old director D. W. Griffith, and famous silent-film star Charlie Chaplin to form their own film company, called United Artists. She also created her own production company to produce their films. As journalist Herbert Howe put it at the time, "No role she can play on the screen is as great as

the role she plays in the motion picture industry. Mary Pickford the actress is completely overshadowed by Mary Pickford the individual."

Thanks to her tireless work ethic, Mary's career was long and rewarding. She continued to act, produce, and direct hit movies, earning herself an Oscar for her first "talkie" (a movie with sound). She and husband Douglas Fairbanks were even the first people to press their hands in cement outside of the famous Grauman's Chinese Theatre. Mary's success is an example to every actor: know what you're worth and what you want, and do what you need to do to get it.

BUT NOT MUCH HAS CHANGED

Actresses today are still fighting for the respect that Mary demanded right out of the gate. She was a savvy businesswoman and knew her worth, which meant she had no problem bouncing from studio to studio to get the money she deserved. After all, she had helped the studios make that money. Even her move from acting to producing and directing is hard for actresses to pull off these days. Men still dominate the industry—and the salaries. Mary is a Hollywood legend not just for her contribution to creating the industry itself, but for being a woman who found a way to do what she loved in the face of sexism and misogyny.

FRIDA KAHLO

ARTIST

BORN: 1907 · DIED: 1954

- Started her groundbreaking career as an artist at age 18 after a tragic accident
- Her suffering led to her success, with honest and emotional artwork

"THE ONLY THING I KNOW IS THAT I PAINT BECAUSE I NEED TO, AND I PAINT WHATEVER PASSES THROUGH MY HEAD WITHOUT ANY OTHER CONSIDERATION." —FRIDA KAHLO

Life has a way of throwing you a curveball the minute you think you have things figured out. Groundbreaking Mexican artist Frida Kahlo discovered that firsthand when a near-fatal bus accident turned her life upside down. But without it, she might never have picked up a paintbrush.

While growing up, Frida enjoyed helping her father in his photography studio, but her true love was science. Getting into the prestigious National Preparatory School in Mexico City when she was 15 brought her one step closer to her ultimate goal of becoming a doctor. She had big plans for her life. But life had even bigger plans for her.

In 1925, her bus collided with a streetcar, sending a metal handrail through her body. Her injuries were so severe that doctors didn't think she'd live through the night: she had multiple fractures of her spine, collarbone, and ribs, a shattered pelvis, a broken foot, and a dislocated shoulder. She did survive, but she never fully recovered, requiring 30 operations throughout a lifetime of poor health.

At 18 years old, Frida was barely able to move and had no hope of completing her medical education. So she taught herself to paint. Not only could she paint from her bed, but her artwork allowed her to vent the pain and frustration she was feeling. Her suffering and her art went hand in hand, as did her success.

Frida became known for her bold, honest paintings—mostly self-portraits expressing her physical and mental agony in

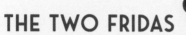

THE TWO FRIDAS

If you've ever felt like you're a different person when you're around certain people, you're not alone! When Frida divorced her husband, Diego Rivera, she felt torn between two versions of herself. She used her talents to explore both sides in a piece she called "The Two Fridas." In the painting, a Frida dressed in traditional European clothing sits next to a second Frida, dressed in modern Mexican Tehuana clothing, on a background of stormy skies. The hearts of both women are exposed and connected to each other. The Mexican Frida belonged to Diego—this was the version of herself that he loved and that bloomed because of their relationship. But European Frida was bleeding, because this was the side of Frida that her husband disliked and wanted her to abandon. Through her art, she embraced both sides of herself.

symbols that others could understand. Between her injuries, her fiery and troubled marriage, and her devastation at not being able to have children, she had a lot to work with. While her work was sometimes shocking and even gruesome, it was some of the most raw, emotional, and relatable work anyone had seen.

Frida's face in her portraits was always stoic, showing clearly the strength that she tapped into to endure her pain. Painting that strength seemed to help her feel it. And her strength helped her paint the truth. Frida's work continues to inspire courage and honesty in artists and art lovers to this day.

"MY PAINTINGS ARE THE MOST FRANK EXPRESSION OF MYSELF, WITHOUT TAKING INTO CONSIDERATION EITHER JUDGMENTS OR PREJUDICES OF ANYONE." —FRIDA KAHLO

Frida never let her physical weakness stop her from doing what she wanted to do. Her father taught her that principle when a childhood struggle with polio left her with impaired leg function. He encouraged her to swim, wrestle, and play soccer—none of which little girls were supposed to do—to help her recover.

Frida's strong, independent spirit helped her throughout her life. When she found herself bedridden and in bad health on the night of her first major solo exhibition in Mexico, she had herself wheeled into the gallery on her bed. The show was a huge success. And when her leg had to be amputated, she refused to be embarrassed. Instead, she wore a red velvet boot covered in bells on the artificial leg. Frida's resilience teaches us that we are all infinitely stronger than we think.

A FIERY SPIRIT

Frida was one of just 35 girls in a school of 2,000 students, but she felt right at home among the boys. Her closest circle of friends called themselves the *cachuchas*, a reference to a spicy Spanish dance. The seven boys and two girls were smart but mischievous, pulling off pranks like riding donkeys through the school hallways.

When she married Diego Rivera at age 22, Frida devoted herself to being a good housewife. She dressed beautifully, cleaned their home, and prepared picnic lunches to bring to Diego at work.

But Frida's marriage was tumultuous, and her independent tom-boy spirit began to shine through again. She smoke and drank like the men and loved watching bloody boxing matches. Despite her broken body, she reveled in dancing the night away. And she threw herself into her work, determined to make a living from it so she didn't have to depend on Diego.

The ill-suited pair divorced, but Diego soon wanted his wife back. They remarried a year later with a new arrangement. Diego wanted Frida to accept his flaws and philandering. She did, but with her own conditions: they would marry as friends—no more—and each would make their own money. She happily returned to taking care of their home but never again lost her independent spirit.

JACKIE MITCHELL

BASEBALL PLAYER

BORN: 1913 · DIED: 1987

- One of the first women to be signed to a minor-league baseball contract
- Struck out baseball legends Babe Ruth and Lou Gehrig when she was 17 years old

"BETTER HITTERS THAN THEM COULDN'T HIT ME. WHY SHOULD THEY'VE BEEN ANY DIFFERENT?"

—JACKIE MITCHELL, ON STRIKING OUT TWO OF BASEBALL'S MOST FAMOUS PLAYERS

Jackie Mitchell's father seemed determined to make a ballplayer out of her. He took her to a baseball diamond as soon as she could walk and taught her to love the game. Jackie learned the finer points of pitching from her neighbor, Charles Arthur "Dazzy" Vance, who just so happened to be a minor-league player and future Baseball Hall of Famer. With that sort of background and plenty of passion and talent, it wasn't long before big names in baseball noticed her.

Joe Engel, president of a minor-league team called the Lookouts, was always searching for new ways to fascinate fans. Especially during the Great Depression, baseball relied on gimmicks and stunts to help fill seats

and entertain the crowds. And Joe was well known in the industry for his showmanship. When he saw Jackie play in the women's league, he knew he needed to sign her. After all, a girl who could strike out her male competition would make headlines.

Joe had already attracted an audience by scheduling two exhibition games featuring the most beloved team in the league, the Yankees. And throwing Jackie into the mix did exactly what he'd hoped—it got the media's attention. Unfortunately for Jackie, most of the headlines were sexist and condescending. They treated her like either a little girl playing dress-up or a pretty girl playing for their affections. Jackie didn't

"GIRL PITCHER FANS RUTH AND GEHRIG" —HEADLINE IN *THE NEW YORK TIMES*

let that rattle her. She even put on a bit of a show for the cameras, applying makeup before the game. She knew her pitching would prove to reporters that she was no joke.

That day, 17-year-old Jackie Mitchell went up against two of the most famous and legendary players in Yankees history: Babe Ruth and Lou Gehrig. The day before the match, Ruth was quoted in *The New York*

Times as saying, "I don't know what's going to happen if they begin to let women in baseball. Of course, they will never make good. Why? Because they are too delicate. It would kill them to play ball every day." Clearly, he didn't think much of his competition. Then Jackie struck him out.

Ruth cursed at the umpire and threw his bat on the ground in a fit of anger. Jackie struck out Gehrig next, but her arm was tired from the effort. Her manager pulled her from the game when she walked the next batter. You might think that Jackie had earned her place in the history books, but she's been mostly forgotten by baseball. Many people considered the whole thing a stunt, saying that Ruth and Gehrig let Jackie strike them out for the publicity.

Hall of Fame research director Tim Wiles doesn't think so. He says, "Even hitters as great as Ruth and Gehrig would be reluctant to admit they'd really been struck out by a 17-year-old girl." And although Ruth held records for his home runs, he also held records for his numerous strikeouts. (He was proof that you can never win if you're afraid to fail.)

THE GREAT DEPRESSION

When the Great Depression began in 1929, people all over the country found themselves jobless, homeless, and hungry. They stood in long lines for free bread and soup provided by charitable organizations, and later by the government. Not only had the economy collapsed, but a drought had swept across the nation and made farming all but impossible. You might think that, in these conditions, people would forget all about diversions like baseball. But the American public needed fun and distraction more than ever. And baseball delivered, with many of the sport's most famous players coming out of the 1930s.

Jackie had no doubt that she had really struck out two of baseball's all-time greats. Just a few years before her death she said, "Better hitters than them couldn't hit me. Why should they've been any different?" But soon after her feat, baseball commissioner Kenesaw Mountain Landis withdrew her contract, saying that the sport was too demanding for women.

At the end of the day, it doesn't matter whether or not Ruth and Gehrig struck out for a stunt. Jackie had faced two of baseball's greatest players. She overcame whatever fear she felt, whatever stereotypes she faced, and she pitched her best. We'll never know whether Jackie herself could have been one of the greats. But we do know she's an inspiration to women, and to female athletes in particular, for standing up to giants.

TRY SOMETHING NEW

The stars seemed to align for Jackie. Her father taught her about baseball when most girls were learning to play with dolls. Then her neighbor, who happened to play ball professionally, taught her his best moves. She loved the sport, and she played it better than the boys.

Not everyone is lucky enough to be introduced to their passion at an early age. That's why you have to try a lot of different hobbies and see what sticks. Take those piano lessons, try playing tennis, go snowboarding with your friend, let your grandma teach you how to knit. You won't know what you love to do until you give it a chance. And if something's not for you, don't feel bad about moving on to the next thing. If you keep trying, you're bound to find something that suits you.

ANNE FRANK

AUTHOR

BORN: 1929 · DIED: 1945

- Kept a diary of her years hiding from the Nazis with her family
- Her courage and optimism were as impressive as her storytelling
- She perished in a concentration camp, but her diary lives on in 67 languages

> "I SEE THE WORLD BEING SLOWLY TRANSFORMED INTO A WILDERNESS; I HEAR THE APPROACHING THUNDER THAT, ONE DAY, WILL DESTROY US TOO. I FEEL THE SUFFERING OF MILLIONS. AND YET, WHEN I LOOK UP AT THE SKY, I SOMEHOW FEEL THAT EVERYTHING WILL CHANGE FOR THE BETTER, THAT THIS CRUELTY TOO SHALL END, THAT PEACE AND TRANQUILITY WILL RETURN ONCE MORE."

—ANNE FRANK, JULY 15, 1944

You've probably studied the Holocaust in school. You've read about the concentration camps, where more than six million Europeans were killed because they were Jewish. You know that Hitler was the man in charge, leading an army of Nazi soldiers to commit terrible crimes against their fellow citizens. But you might not know how it all started.

Germany's economy was at its weakest point after the Germans lost World War I, and the German people were looking for someone to blame. Enter: a charismatic politician named Adolf Hitler. Hitler convinced crowd after crowd that the Jews were responsible for their unemployment, poverty, and strife.

ANNE'S SHORT LIFE

Anne Frank was born in a restless and dangerous time for Frankfurt, Germany. When Adolf Hitler came to power in 1933, her father knew it was time to leave. He moved Anne with her mother and older sister, Margot, to Amsterdam, the Netherlands. The Franks enjoyed a relatively normal life until Germany invaded the Netherlands. Jews like Anne were forced to go to separate schools and to wear the Star of David so they could be identified at a glance.

When Margot received a notice to report to a Nazi work camp, the family hurried into hiding. An annex, accessed by a hidden staircase behind a bookcase, became their home for the next two years. Until the Nazis came for them and took them to various concentration camps, their only contact with the outside world was a handful of loyal friends who risked their own lives to bring food and clothing.

Only Anne's father survived the Holocaust. Anne, her mother, and her sister all died from illness in the spring of 1945, just weeks before the English arrived to liberate Anne's camp. When Otto Frank read his daughter's diary (found and kept safe by a friend), he set out to fulfill one of the wishes it contained: that her story be published.

It's hard to imagine an entire country being so gullible, and so willing to commit violence against their own for the false hope of financial recovery. But that's why a 14-year-old Jewish girl named Anne Frank is so important. Her diary, written over the course of two years in hiding from the Nazis, gives us a window into life during the Holocaust and the hardships suffered by Jewish people long before they arrived at concentration camps.

Anne put a human face on a crisis so atrocious and so immense that we would otherwise have a hard time wrapping our heads around it. And understanding that piece of history through her eyes ensures that we don't repeat it—that we speak up against hatred, violence, and oppression and never let it get to the point of harming people again. But the fact that she wrote a diary doesn't make her a trailblazer. How she wrote it does.

The Diary of a Young Girl has been published in 67 languages not just because it's a historical document, but because it's a thoughtful, well-written narrative. Anne, who dreamed of being a writer, had even begun to rewrite the diary as a novel so that she could someday publish it. She chronicled not just the physical sensations of sharing what amounted to a very small apartment with her family and four other people, but also the very normal emotions of a teenage girl, and the hopes and fears of a young women in a country at war.

Inside the relative comfort of the annex, Anne and the others lived every day in fear. They couldn't open windows during the day because someone might see. They couldn't speak or move too loudly because someone might hear. They held their breath when someone approached until they knew if it was a friend delivering food or the Nazis coming to take them. The small space, which would have been livable if they were occasionally allowed to leave it, was suffocating in its isolation.

But through all that, Anne retained her optimism. She wrote entries like this one, the most famous of all: "It's really a wonder that I haven't dropped all my ideals, because they seem so absurd and impossible to carry out. Yet I keep them, because in spite of everything, I still believe that people are really good at heart." Anne had faith that people would overcome the worst in themselves and defeat the Nazis, even if she didn't live to see it happen.

TELL YOUR STORY

Have you ever had a hard time getting an adult to take you seriously? Felt like you have to meet an age requirement to have an opinion? When an adult shuts you down, you might be tempted to just keep quiet in the future. But don't let anyone discourage you from sharing your thoughts and ideas. Anne had this to say about it in her diary: "Although I'm only fourteen, I know quite well what I want. I know who is right and who is wrong. I have my opinions, my own ideas and principles, and although it might sound pretty mad from an adolescent, I feel more of a person than a child, I feel quite independent of anyone." Anne was wise beyond her years, but it was  her confidence in her own abilities that allowed her to share her story. And hers was a story the world needed to hear.

Anne wrote her diary as a testament to the human race and our ability to improve ourselves and our surroundings. In it, she wrote, "Parents can only give good advice or put them on the right paths, but the final forming of a person's character lies in their own hands." Her belief in her own strength, in humanity, and in doing the right thing lives on in her writing and encourages us to find the same in ourselves.

BARBARA JOHNS

CIVIL RIGHTS ACTIVIST

BORN: 1935 · DIED: 1991

- Organized a peaceful protest against segregation when she was 16
- Her protest was one of the foundational pieces of the lawsuit that ended segregation in U.S. schools

"CHANGE IN THIS COMMONWEALTH AND THIS COUNTRY HAS ALWAYS COME WHEN BRAVE INDIVIDUALS STAND UP AND DEMAND THEIR RIGHTS, AND SO OFTEN IT HAS BEEN A YOUNG PERSON WHO CAN STILL SEE INJUSTICE WITH CLEAR EYES. TO ME, THAT'S THE LEGACY OF BARBARA JOHNS—A BRAVE YOUNG WOMAN WHO STOOD UP AND DEMANDED THE RIGHTS THAT THE CONSTITUTION GUARANTEED TO HER AND TO EACH OF US." —FORMER GOVERNOR OF VIRGINIA TERRY MCAULIFFE

Barbara Johns had three strikes against her when she decided to fight for a better education in the era of segregation: she was female, she was black, and she was 16 years old. Just one of those attributes was enough to make people disregard you in 1951—having all three practically guaranteed you a spot in the background of whatever was happening. But Barbara's outspoken uncle, Vernon Johns, had always taught her to stand up for what she believed in. And she believed that students deserved a better education than they were receiving at Robert Russa Monton High School.

While white students attended a well-equipped high school, black students had hand-me-down equipment and books, when they had any at all. Although the school was built to hold 150 students, the hallways swelled with more than 400. In response to complaints, the school board built tarpaper shacks (which are exactly what they sound like—shacks made from construction-grade paper) to hold the overflow. The ceilings leaked when it rained, and students had to wear coats in winter for lack of heat.

A GOOD INFLUENCE

Barbara's uncle, Vernon Johns, was a prominent minister and a pioneer of the civil rights movement. He led by example and made sure that his nieces and nephews grew curious about black history. Knowing she had such a strong role model in her life gives us a little insight into the roots of Barbara's natural leadership abilities.

Some might consider Vernon a bad influence for encouraging his niece to stir up trouble. But it's always good to have people around you who inspire you to think outside the box. If you have someone in your life who makes you ask questions and get involved in your community, consider yourself lucky!

So she organized a peaceful protest—the country's first recorded walk-out, in fact. The school's principal received a phone call telling him that students were causing trouble downtown, which got him out of the way. Then the teachers received a notice about a schoolwide assembly. When they arrived with their students, Barbara appeared on stage and asked the teachers to wait outside.

Alone with the student body, Barbara gave an impassioned speech about the unreasonable state of their school. She argued that a student strike would make the school board realize the need for improvements. Barbara passed out posters covered with catchy slogans, and all 400 students went outside to picket.

But instead of seeing reason, the superintendent dismissed the students' claims and said their school was as good as any other in the county. Feeling outraged and powerless, Barbara contacted the NAACP (the National Association for the Advancement of Colored People). The organization sent over two lawyers who discussed options with the students. The outcome was a lawsuit aimed at ending segregation.

Although they lost that lawsuit (*Davis v. Prince Edward*), it became part of *Brown v. Board of Education*, the famous suit that did

"IT SEEMED LIKE REACHING FOR THE MOON."

–BARBARA JOHNS

end segregation in the United States three years later. It took a long time for Barbara and her fellow students to be credited with contributing to this monumental change in our country's history. Author Taylor Branch had a guess as to the reason: "The idea that non-adults of any race might play a leading role in political events had simply failed to register on anyone."

But that's no longer the case. Former Virginia governor Terry McAuliffe named one of the state's buildings after Barbara. His 2017 press release read, "When Barbara stood up for equal access to education as a plaintiff in the case of *Brown v. Board of Education*, she helped changed the history of our nation for the better and inspired a new generation of civil rights leaders." Although Barbara retired to a quiet life in Pennsylvania, her legacy of leadership rings loudly through history.

CLAUDETTE COLVIN

CIVIL RIGHTS ACTIVIST

BORN: 1939

- Kept her seat on a segregated bus at 15, a full nine months before Rosa Parks
- Testified in the court case that ended the segregated bus system

"I KNEW THEN AND I KNOW NOW THAT, WHEN IT COMES TO JUSTICE, THERE IS NO EASY WAY TO GET IT. YOU CAN'T SUGARCOAT IT. YOU HAVE TO TAKE A STAND AND SAY, 'THIS IS NOT RIGHT.'" —CLAUDETTE COLVIN

If you're a teenager, you probably catch a lot of flak from your parents. Maybe you rolled your eyes at them or let a sarcastic comment slip. You're not the first, and you won't be the last. Teens spend a lot of time testing their boundaries, which happens to be how they grow into smart, creative, engaged adults. (OK, not always. But usually.)

Sometimes, "testing boundaries" means staying out past curfew. Sometimes it means questioning authority. You just have to figure out how far you're willing to go, and whether it's worth the trouble. 15-year-old Claudette Colvin questioned authority and ended up in handcuffs, but what she did changed everything.

The year was 1955, and Claudette had been studying black leaders like Harriet Tubman and Sojourner Truth in school. Discussions turned to the abuses black Americans faced under Jim Crow laws that forced them to always be second to, and separate from, white people. They couldn't sit at the counter in a restaurant or try on clothes in a store. Black and white students went to separate schools. On public buses, black riders had to stand or sit in the back of the bus as well as give up their seat to any white person who wanted it.

On March 2nd, 1955, Claudette refused to give up her seat on a bus in Montgomery, Alabama. When asked why in a later interview, she replied, "My head was just

too full of black history, you know, the oppression that we went through. It felt like Sojourner Truth was on one side pushing down, and Harriet Tubman was on the other side of me pushing me down. I couldn't get up." She knew in her gut that staying seated was the right thing to do.

But it certainly wasn't the easy thing to do. The police officers who dragged her off the bus harassed her, and she was taken straight to a cell in the women's jail. She had no idea if anyone knew she was missing or where she was. Thankfully, friends who had witnessed the arrest alerted Claudette's mother, who found her kneeling in the middle of the jail cell, crying and praying.

Neighbors embraced her when she got home; they were happy she was safe and they were proud of her actions. But she knew the trouble she might have caused for them. She said in her biography, *Claudette Colvin: Twice Toward Justice*, "I had stood up to a white bus driver and two white cops. I had challenged the bus law. There had been lynchings and cross burnings for that kind of thing…. Probably nobody on King Hill slept that night." Her actions

THE GOLDEN RULES

There are a few golden rules to keep in mind when rebelling: If you're going to talk back, make sure you know what you're talking about. Think things through. Disagree respectfully. You're entitled to your opinion, but so is everyone else.

Claudette had just studied the laws she challenged, she knew her rights, and she understood the consequences of her actions. She made a thoughtful choice to peacefully protest something she felt was wrong.

scared as many people as they inspired, and parents started warning their children to stay away from her at school. The simple act of keeping her seat was enough to put everyone's life in danger.

Claudette pled not guilty to assault and battery, disorderly conduct, and defying the segregation law. She was found guilty anyway and received probation for her crimes. While the punishment was light, the unfair ruling fanned her desire to keep fighting. She was a key witness in *Browder v. Gayle*, the 1956 court case that ended the segregated bus system.

Change happens slowly and in small increments. While Claudette might not be as famous as Rosa Parks for keeping her seat that day in Alabama, she absolutely changed the world with her small act of courage and desire to make a difference.

COURAGEOUS COPYCAT

You may have heard of Rosa Parks, the woman who famously refused to give up her seat to a white person on a Montgomery, Alabama, bus and was arrested for it. She's also credited as one of the great heroines of the civil rights movement for doing so.

It turns out that Rosa may have gotten her inspiration from Claudette Colvin. Working as a secretary for the NAACP (the National Association for the Advancement of Colored People) in the same area, Rosa was well aware of Claudette. The NAACP decided that Rosa was a more sympathetic figure than poor, dark-skinned, 15-year-old Claudette. So Rosa took her cue from Claudette just nine months later and elevated the civil rights movement.

ELIZABETH ECKFORD

CIVIL RIGHTS ICON

BORN: 1941

- Became an unintentional icon of the civil rights movement at 15
- Was one of the first black students integrated into a white school in Arkansas
- Conquered trauma and depression to bring hope to students

> "IF WE HAVE HONESTLY ACKNOWLEDGED OUR PAINFUL BUT SHARED PAST, THEN WE CAN HAVE RECONCILIATION." —ELIZABETH ECKFORD

When we think of a trailblazer, we often think of someone who devoted his or her life to a cause. But sometimes a single moment of courage can get the job done. Elizabeth Eckford's moment was captured in one of the most iconic images of the civil rights movement.

The black-and-white photograph shows 15-year-old Elizabeth walking to school on a hot September morning in 1957, followed by an angry mob of students and several members of the Arkansas National Guard. In a white cotton shirtdress and sunglasses, she looks straight ahead as she carries her notebook toward the school. She assumes the soldiers are there to protect her, but when she gets to the doors, they bar her from entering instead.

Elizabeth was one of a group called the Little Rock Nine—the first nine black students in Arkansas to attend a white school. The Supreme Court had ordered that all schools be integrated, but some southern states were slow to comply. The Little Rock school board decided to spread integration out over a period of years. When the board was finally forced to admit black students to Little Rock Central High School, the governor called in the Guard. It would take the president of the United States sending in the 101st Airborne as an escort to get those nine students into the school.

On that first day, Elizabeth was all alone. The other students had planned to arrive together with a handful of adults. But Elizabeth's family didn't own a phone, so she arrived by bus and walked the two blocks to the school unaccompanied. When the soldiers barred her from entering, she thought she had the wrong entrance.

Finally, a soldier pointed across the street, and she understood that they weren't going to let her in.

Sad and scared, she started walking back to the bus stop when she realized that a crowd of people were following her. A mixture of students and adults were nipping at her heels, yelling profane suggestions, death threats, and racial slurs. Will Counts took his iconic photograph during that walk back to the bus stop. It has served, ever since, as a reminder of the horrors of racism and segregation, and the hardships faced in getting to where we are today. (We still have a long way to go in dealing with these issues.)

Although Elizabeth and the other students were eventually allowed into the school, the cruel treatment at the hands of other students didn't stop. Eventually, Little Rock closed all of their high schools to avoid full-scale integration, and Elizabeth finished her credits elsewhere. The events of that school year left Elizabeth in a deep depression

SEPARATE BUT EQUAL

Imagine walking through a town and seeing signs everywhere telling you where you were allowed to sit, stand, talk, or eat based on your hair color. You have to look for signs that say "blondes only" because it's illegal for you to use the "brunettes only" restroom. That was the reality of segregation in America, right up until the Supreme Court ruled it unconstitutional in schools with *Brown v. Board of Education* in 1954.

Of course, the signs didn't actually refer to hair color. They referred to skin color. A black person could be arrested for using a water fountain marked "whites only." Because the 14th Amendment guarantees black Americans equal rights, the segregation loophole was referred to as "separate but equal." But the facilities designated for black people were hardly equal, if they existed at all.

that would take years of therapy, medication, and introspection to shake.

Elizabeth's courage and hopefulness on that September day in 1957 changed Little Rock forever. Her composure in the face of atrocious hatred is frozen in time, forever associated with that period of excruciating change. And now that she's clawed her way through the trauma and fought her way back from depression, she offers a message to today's students: education is its own reward, strength and shyness can coexist, and compassion can save lives.

"I EXPECTED THAT THERE MAY BE SOMETHING MORE AVAILABLE TO ME AT CENTRAL THAT WAS NOT AVAILABLE AT DUNBAR; THAT THERE MIGHT BE MORE COURSES I COULD PURSUE; THAT THERE WERE MORE OPTIONS AVAILABLE. I WAS NOT PREPARED FOR WHAT ACTUALLY HAPPENED." –ELIZABETH ECKFORD

SUSAN ELOISE HINTON

AUTHOR

BORN: 1948

- Wrote *The Outsiders*, which still sells 500 thousand copies per year, when she was 17
- Continues to have a successful writing career, with six novels, one book of short stories, and two children's books

> "IT SEEMED FUNNY TO ME THAT THE SUNSET SHE SAW FROM HER PATIO AND THE ONE I SAW FROM THE BACK STEPS WAS THE SAME ONE. MAYBE THE TWO DIFFERENT WORLDS WE LIVED IN WEREN'T SO DIFFERENT. WE SAW THE SAME SUNSET."

– S. E. HINTON, *THE OUTSIDERS*

When you think of an author, who do you picture? Maybe someone older? Someone who looks like they give lectures at a college and respond to "Professor"? Maybe you picture someone like J. K. Rowling—lovely and smart, encouraging in a motherly way. But you probably don't picture a high school student.

We have this perception that people do great things later in life. Sure, occasionally you hear about a tech genius who started his company in his mother's garage when he was 19. But it normally takes years, even decades, of education and life experience to get to the top of your game. Doesn't it?

Not always. Susan Eloise Hinton (known as S. E. Hinton) wrote one of the most read, most assigned,

"ANYTHING YOU READ CAN INFLUENCE YOUR WORK, SO I TRY TO READ GOOD STUFF." —S.E. HINTON

and most influential books in history—*The Outsiders*—when she was just 17 years old. In fact, she used her Oklahoma high school as inspiration for the novel, which is a story about the clash of two rival cliques divided by money and status.

To this day, *The Outsiders* sells 500 thousand copies per year—more than 14 million copies have sold over its lifetime. It was even adapted into a 1983 film starring A-list actors like Rob Lowe and Tom Cruise. Hinton is also credited with establishing the genre of Young Adult Fiction, which is a pretty big deal. Without it, we wouldn't have books like *The Hunger Games*, *The Perks of Being a Wallflower*, or *The Giver*.

Any author would be proud of those accomplishments, but Susan noticed one more: "*The Outsiders* is definitely my best-selling book; but what I like most about it is how it has taught a lot of kids to enjoy reading." While she went on to write better books (she worked hard to improve her writing), none was as beloved as *The Outsiders*.

HIDDEN IN PLAIN SIGHT

Many female authors use their initials to avoid being pigeonholed by male readers, and Susan's publisher suggested she do the same. After her first book became a hit, she continued using her initials because she liked the privacy it afforded her.

She wasn't the first writer to prefer to stay behind the scenes. In fact, introversion is a common trait among literary figures. Famous authors like J. D. Salinger and Harper Lee have all enjoyed life away from the limelight.

We tend to put authors up on a pedestal, but they're just people with a story to tell. As Susan says, "A writer's life is not very exciting. Usually you're alone in a room with your tools—paper, pen, imagination. I walk the dog, ride my horse, wander the grocery store wondering what to cook for dinner." Maybe it's not exciting, but it does sound pretty great.

If you're someone who has always dreamed of writing the next Great American Novel, it's also excellent news. Yours isn't some lofty, unachievable goal. Writing is a matter of hard work and imagination. You can start telling your story any time you choose. Why not today?

"I'VE BEEN WRITING PRACTICALLY SINCE I LEARNED TO READ. SO BY THE TIME I WROTE *THE OUTSIDERS*, I'D BEEN WRITING FOR ABOUT EIGHT YEARS. IT WASN'T LIKE, 'OH, ALL OF A SUDDEN I'M 15 YEARS OLD AND STARTED WRITING A BOOK.' IT WAS ACTUALLY THE THIRD BOOK I'D WRITTEN. IT'S JUST THE FIRST ONE I EVER TRIED TO GET PUBLISHED." —S.E. HINTON

SAMANTHA REED SMITH

PEACE ACTIVIST AND GOODWILL AMBASSADOR

BORN: 1972 · DIED: 1985

- Wrote letters to the leader of the Soviet Union and his ambassador when she was 10

- Acted as a goodwill ambassador between the United States and the Soviet Union

> "EVERYONE IN THE SOVIET UNION WHO HAS KNOWN SAMANTHA SMITH WILL FOREVER REMEMBER THE IMAGE OF THE AMERICAN GIRL WHO, LIKE MILLIONS OF SOVIET YOUNG MEN AND WOMEN, DREAMT ABOUT PEACE, AND ABOUT FRIENDSHIP BETWEEN THE PEOPLES OF THE UNITED STATES AND THE SOVIET UNION."

—MIKHAIL GORBACHEV, FORMER PRESIDENT OF THE SOVIET UNION

When you watch the news today, it's easy to think that the bad is starting to crowd out the good. You might see stories about hurricanes wreaking havoc, terror attacks on tourists, or unpredictable countries advertising their nuclear arsenal. It's scary, and it can make anyone feel small and helpless. But there's always a way to make a difference, right where you are.

In 1982, two of the world's most powerful nations were threatening each other with nuclear war. What could anyone do but wait and worry? That's when a 10-year-old girl from Maine decided to take matters into her own hands.

Samantha Smith and her mom had been reading an article in *Time* magazine about the new leader of the Soviet Union, Yuri Andropov. The article talked about the arms race, in which the United States and the Soviet Union competed to develop nuclear weapons. People didn't know what to expect from Andropov: would he push his country to win the race, or would he be a voice of reason and calm things down?

THE LITTLE PICTURE

When you read headlines about other countries, you tend to see them as a whole. You don't often stop and imagine the people who live in those countries—people just like you, your friends, your family. Those people are also reading the news, worrying about the world, and feeling like there's nothing they can do. But for a moment in the early 1980s, Samantha Smith changed that. She made the world see things from a human perspective, rather than a global one. While understanding the big picture is good, sometimes you have to zoom in and look at the details.

Samantha didn't want to wait for an answer. She had read about nuclear bombs—they were the most destructive weapons ever created. With her mom's help, she wrote a letter to Andropov introducing herself, congratulating him on his new job, and asking him a simple question: "Are you going vote to have a war, or not?"

Her message reached not just the man in charge but also his citizens when it was published in the Soviet newspaper, *Pravda*, the following spring. But Samantha was puzzled that she didn't hear from Andropov directly, so she wrote to the Soviet ambassador to the United States, Anatoly Dobrynin. In a long response, he assured Samantha that the Soviet Union had no desire to use nuclear weapons. "We want peace for ourselves and for all peoples of the planet. For our children and for you, Samantha," he wrote. And then he invited her to see that first hand.

That July, Samantha and her family enjoyed two weeks as Andropov's guests in the Soviet Union, touring famous Russian cities Moscow and Leningrad (now Saint Petersburg). She even spent five days at a children's summer camp called Artek, where she joined Soviet children in activities like swimming and dancing. The smiley, blue-eyed girl gave Soviets a more realistic idea of what Americans looked

and acted like, and the press coverage she received gave Americans a peek into what Soviets looked and acted like.

When Samantha died in a plane crash two years later, both nations mourned the loss. More than a thousand people attended her funeral. The Soviet Union named a postage stamp, a diamond, a mountain, and an asteroid after her. The state of Maine declared the first Monday in June Samantha Smith Day. A life-size statue of Samantha with a bear at her feet (a symbol for the Soviet Union) releasing a dove (a symbol of peace) still stands at the entrance of the Maine State Museum.

Artek also honors her with a memorial garden of olive trees (the olive branch is a symbol of peace) and activities that focus on promoting unity. Former camp counselor Valery Kostin still remembers her and says, "We need to tell them about the little girl from Maine who changed the world with her smile and her simple message of peace." Samantha was technically a preteen trailblazer and her life was tragically short, but she made an impact so big that the world still feels it.

ALEX'S LEMONADE STAND

Preteen trailblazer Alex Scott was diagnosed with cancer before she turned one year old. Although she knew that she wouldn't survive, she wanted to do something to help kids like her beat the odds. She started her famous lemonade stand when she was four years old (with the help of her older brother) and raised $2,000.

Alex lost her battle when she was eight years old, but her lemonade stands had already raised more than a million dollars to help find a cure for her disease. The foundation created in her name continues to raise money for the cause. Alex and Samantha are both shining examples of what former American president Theodore Roosevelt said: "Do what you can, with what you have, where you are."

So the next time you're feeling helpless, think about Samantha's letter. What can you do right now to make a difference? You can coordinate a canned-food drive in your neighborhood to help hungry families, or volunteer to cuddle cats and walk dogs at your local shelter. When a natural disaster strikes, you can help your family and friends clean out their closets and donate clothing and household items to people who lost theirs. Your actions might feel like a drop of water in the ocean, but they can have big ripple effects.

EMMA WATSON

ACTRESS AND ACTIVIST

BORN: 1990

- Accomplished actress who has brought to life strong female characters
- Named UN Women Goodwill Ambassador (youngest in history) in 2014
- Advocates for gender equality through the HeForShe and Time's Up campaigns

"IT'S NOT THE ABSENCE OF FEAR, IT'S OVERCOMING IT. SOMETIMES YOU'VE GOT TO BLAST THROUGH AND HAVE FAITH." —EMMA WATSON

As the smart and fearless Hermione Granger in eight *Harry Potter* movies or as an accomplished human rights activist in real life, Emma Watson is someone every girl can look up to. Her love of learning is contagious, and her confidence and courage are magnetic on screen and off. But she'll be the first one to tell you that she feels anything but fearless.

Emma landed the role of a lifetime when she was just nine years old. J. K. Rowling's *Harry Potter* is the best-selling book series of all time—there's hardly a muggle in the world who hasn't read about "The Boy Who Lived." That meant that Emma had quite a lot to live up to, but she didn't let fear stop her from pursuing her calling. She worked hard to develop her skills and has continued to captivate audiences in movies like *The Perks of Being a Wallflower* and Disney's *Beauty and the Beast.*

Since leaving the wizarding world, Emma has dedicated herself to making a difference for women in the real world. At 19 years old, she started working with People Tree, a fashion brand that makes clothing out of environmentally friendly materials and promises to

"YOUNG GIRLS ARE TOLD THAT YOU HAVE TO BE THE DELICATE PRINCESS. HERMIONE TAUGHT THEM THAT YOU CAN BE THE WARRIOR." –EMMA WATSON

EDUCATION FIRST

Much like Hermione, Emma always turned to education as the first line of defense against her anxiety. She made up for a lack of experience with research and reading. The more she learned, the more comfortable she felt.

When most people would have ridden the wave of fame and fortune that came with acting in a hugely popular movie series, Emma put her education first. She scheduled filming around her classes, and she made the time to attend and graduate from Brown University—one of the most prestigious schools in the United States.

When she realized how passionate she was about feminist and humanitarian work, Emma felt tempted to pursue a master's degree to prepare her for her next steps. Then she realized that she was already learning more than a master's could teach her from rolling up her sleeves and getting involved. But, in true Hermione fashion, she still assigned herself one book per week to help her feel informed.

pay workers fairly. She also traveled to Zambia to work with Camfed (a nonprofit organization that educates and empowers girls in Africa) and to Uruguay to encourage women to get involved in male-dominated politics.

Just a few months after graduating from Brown, Emma found herself face to face with another huge opportunity. UN Women, an organization that advocates for gender equality all over the world, named her their youngest Goodwill Ambassador. Her first assignment was a speech at the United Nations headquarters in New York to announce the HeForShe campaign, and she was terrified.

Although Emma had written the speech herself and gone over it a thousand times, she felt unqualified to give it. She says, "The night before I gave my speech at the UN, I was an emotional wreck. I thought I was going to hyperventilate." But then she realized that it wasn't her experience that made her perfect for the job, it was her passion for the subject of gender equality and her willingness to learn more about it. Emma's nervousness subsided after a few minutes, and her speech (like most things she's applied herself to) was a huge success.

Emma has become not just a world-renowned actress but also a champion for intellect and equality—all before turning 25. Everything she has achieved has been in spite of her fear and anxiety. As she puts it, "No one likes feeling vulnerable and uncomfortable and weak. But I really have found that it's in those moments when I go there that there's a kind of magic." And after all, Emma is the expert on magic. So the next time you feel nervous or scared, know that you're like Emma, and that success is just on the other side of fear.

"ASK YOURSELF IF NOT ME, WHO? IF NOT NOW, WHEN?"

—EMMA WATSON

CAMPAIGNING FOR GENDER EQUALITY

While Emma is a champion for many causes, the one she feels most passionate in pursuing is gender equality. The HeForShe campaign she announced in her speech at the UN invites men to think of themselves as feminists and get involved in advocating for women. It also calls for an end to gender stereotypes that say men can't be sensitive and women can't be strong. Emma believes that breaking down these barriers is the first step in leveling the playing field. That's why she's also a vocal supporter of the Time's Up movement, which calls for an end to sexual assault, harassment, and inequality in the workplace.

Emma wants everyone—men, women, and teens—to get involved in creating solutions to gender inequality. If you don't know exactly how to help, you can take comfort in knowing Emma was unsure at first, too. She said in her speech, "I don't know if I am qualified to be here. All I know is that I care about this problem. And I want to make it better." And that's what matters. That's how you start: decide that you want to help.

TAVI GEVINSON

FASHIONISTA AND WRITER

BORN: 1996

- Started a blog at age 11 that catapulted her into the exclusive world of high-end fashion
- Started an online magazine at 15 that encourages girls to find their own answers

"I AM HAPPIEST AS A SET OF EYES, AND MY GOAL WHENEVER I GO INTO A MOVIE OR ALBUM OR BOOK IS TO LOSE MYSELF IN THE STORY AND FIND MYSELF ON THE WAY OUT." —TAVI GEVINSON

Connecting with other people and places has never been so easy. But there are downsides to all of that access: scrolling through social media can make you feel like you're the only one who doesn't have life figured out. Friends and celebrities alike share their best moments, biggest achievements, amazing vacations, and picture-perfect relationships. You start thinking, "That's great for them, but what about me?"

Tavi Gevinson is one of those girls whose list of accomplishments could make anyone feel like a slacker. She started her fashion blog, Style Rookie, when she was just 11

years old and soon had 50 thousand views per day. By the time she was a teenager, she was being invited to fashion shows all around the world.

At age 14, she was named one of Barbie's Ten Women to Watch. She wrote articles for big-name brands like *Harper's Bazaar* and Barneys.com. Lady Gaga called her "the future of journalism." And by age 15, she was (and still is) the editor-in-chief of her very own online magazine, *Rookie*.

But Tavi will tell you she's still figuring it out.

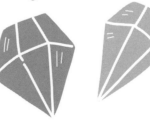

> ## "YOU DON'T NEED TO BE A COMPLETELY COMPLETE HUMAN RIGHT NOW. THAT'S WHAT MAKES YOU HUMAN."
>
> –TAVI GEVINSON

BE TRUE TO YOU

Tavi is what you might call "multipassionate"—she pursues many interests simultaneously. She loves making music and acting as much as she does writing and editing. And she's a firm believer that you don't have to pick just one thing. She's acted in TV shows and movies, as well as in Broadway plays, all while making sure her magazine keeps the topical content coming. With parents who encouraged her creativity and a strong, independent spirit of her own, she's one of the lucky few who never had to be told "just be yourself." She has always marched to the beat of her own drum. And she's made it her mission to help other girls do the same.

And that's exactly what her magazine is all about—teenage girls finding their footing in life. *Rookie*'s articles, many of which are written by teenagers, talk as much about flaws and awkwardness as they do about strengths and feminism. She wants her site to be real and relatable, showing girls that it's OK to be their complicated selves.

Tavi wants girls to discover themselves along the way, rather than rush into being the person they think they *should* be. For her, publishing *Rookie* isn't about having all the answers or providing the answers to others. It's about encouraging girls to find their own answers. She wants you to give yourself permission to change and to try new things and "see what sticks."

"IF THE NEXT THING I DO IS NOT NECESSARILY FILLING THE ROLE OF 'THE FUTURE OF JOURNALISM,' IT'LL PROBABLY BE WHATEVER IS MAKING ME HAPPIEST, AND THAT'S ENOUGH FOR ME." —TAVI GEVINSON

What has stuck for Tavi is a desire to affect social change. She is a feminist, and she feels a responsibility to use her platform for good. When she reads comments from girls who feel like they're not making enough of an impact, Tavi says she wants to reply, "Dude, I ran a fashion blog before I started talking about or wanting to write about anything at all related to social justice." She adds that "change is slow and hard." In other words, we all get there in our own time.

Tavi's aware of the stomach-sinking feeling that social media can give you when you see people like her getting things done. As someone who is deeply familiar with the marketing algorithms used by those sites, she's quick to remind users that the stories they see don't reflect real life—even her own. She says, "You're doing great. Nothing exciting is happening over here except ambitious people in a constant state of panic. Including me."

There's no such thing as a perfect life or an overnight success. Tavi's achievements have been the product of enthusiasm, hard work, patience, and luck. She's a great example of following your inner compass one step at a time, and not letting what others think get in the way. ROOKIE

MALALA YOUSAFZAI

EDUCATION ACTIVIST

BORN: 1997

- Made it her life's mission at the age of 12 to help girls get access to education
- Was shot by the Taliban for publicly speaking out against them
- Recovered and went right back to fighting for girls' education
- Became the youngest person in history to win a Nobel Peace Prize

> "WHEN THE WHOLE WORLD IS SILENT, EVEN ONE VOICE BECOMES POWERFUL." —MALALA YOUSAFZAI

Some days, all you want to do is hit the snooze button, skip school, and spend the day watching TV in your pajamas. But imagine not being allowed to go to school at all—just because you're a girl. That's what Malala Yousafzai faced when the Taliban (a violent political group) took over her hometown.

Malala was born in Swat, Pakistan, to progressive parents who worked hard to give her every opportunity a son would have in a country that favors boys. Her childhood was filled with reading and play, and her father's promise of education and equality.

But everything changed when the Taliban arrived in 2007. In an effort to control the

THE BEAUTY OF SWAT VALLEY

Before the Taliban arrived, Swat Valley was known as "the Switzerland of Asia" and one of the most beautiful valleys in the world. Imagine snow-capped mountains, forests full of evergreens, lush fields, and crystal-blue waters. People from all over the world traveled there to vacation and hike. By 2017, Swat was beginning to open up to tourists again, but the threat of the Taliban still hung in the air. Malala's father described Swat as "paradise lost."

people of Swat, they banned things like music, TV, and shopping. The punishment for defying their laws was death.

THE VALUE OF SUPPORT

Without the love and support of strong parents, Malala may never have received or fought for her education. One Swat teacher said that Ziauddin (an educator himself) "encouraged Malala to speak freely and learn everything she could." In fact, blogging for the BBC was his idea.

When people in your life help you achieve your dreams—even in little ways—remember to thank them. That help might make all the difference!

BBC When the Taliban barred girls from attending school, Malala decided to fight for her right to an education. In 2008, she found her voice and began blogging for the BBC under the pen name "Gul Makai" (the heroine of a local folktale), documenting life under Taliban rule.

Malala described her anxiety as friends and classmates disappeared from school, afraid to return. She wrote about wearing plain clothes rather than the school uniform or her favorite hot-pink outfit to avoid being noticed by the Taliban. Despite her fears, she was determined to attend school. As people started to take an interest in this young girl's powerful writing, the world started to pay attention to the dire situation the Taliban had created.

Even when she and a million others were driven out of their homes by the war between the Taliban and the Pakistani military, Malala continued to fight for education. In 2009, she and her father, Ziauddin, were featured in a *New York Times* documentary about their experience. They spoke openly about their love for learning and for Swat, and against the Taliban.

By 2011, the military had regained control of Swat and girls were finally allowed to return to school. Malala won Pakistan's first National Youth Peace Prize for her work on their behalf. (The award has since been renamed the "National Malala Peace Prize.") But as her voice grew stronger, so did her risk. The Taliban had retreated to more remote areas, but they now knew who Malala was, and they wanted to keep her quiet. In 2012, when she was just 15 years old, a masked gunman forced his way onto Malala's school bus, asked for her by name, and shot her in the head.

By some miracle, the bullet traveled down her neck instead of through her skull. She was airlifted to two different hospitals for

"IF ONE MAN CAN DESTROY EVERYTHING, WHY CAN'T ONE GIRL CHANGE IT?" —MALALA YOUSAFZAI

treatment and multiple surgeries while millions of people around the world waited and prayed for her survival. But Malala didn't just survive the shooting—she recovered and went right back to raising her voice against injustice. She said of the time, "I told myself: Malala, you have already faced death. This is your second life. Don't be afraid. If you are afraid, you can't move forward."

And move forward she did! At age 16, Malala (and her father) created the Malala Fund, an organization dedicated to giving all girls access to education. That same year, she spoke at the United Nations, where her birthday (July 12th) was declared "Malala Day." At 17, she became the youngest person in history to win the Nobel Peace Prize. At 18, she used the Malala Fund to open a school for Syrian refugee girls in Lebanon. And she's just getting started.

In her book, *I Am Malala*, she reminds us that "One child, one teacher, one book, one pen can change the world." So, the next time you want to bury your head in your pillow

rather than in your books, remember what Malala teaches: education is our most powerful weapon.

"WE WERE SCARED, BUT OUR FEAR WAS NOT AS STRONG AS OUR COURAGE." —MALALA YOUSAFZAI

MALALA TODAY

Malala and her family found a permanent home in England after she was shot. The move doesn't just afford them more freedom, it ensures their safety. If they go back to Pakistan, they will continue to be targeted by the Taliban. Today, Malala is studying philosophy, politics, and economics at Oxford University. She wants to get the best education possible so that she can help as many people as possible.

KATIE STAGLIANO

HUNGER ACTIVIST

BORN: 1999

- Started a community garden to help feed families in need in her community
- Supports kids throughout the country in creating their own community gardens

"AT THE AGE OF NINE, I DID NOT HAVE A TRUE UNDERSTANDING OF THE COMPLEXITIES OF THE ISSUE OF HUNGER. WHAT I DID UNDERSTAND WAS THAT THERE WERE INDIVIDUALS AND FAMILIES IN MY COMMUNITY WHO DID NOT HAVE ENOUGH TO EAT." —KATIE STAGLIANO

Everyone has a friend who knows exactly what she wants to do with the rest of her life. She makes figuring it out look easy. But those who are born with passion are few and far between. Most people figure things out as they go. They happen upon an opportunity that leads to a career they love. Or they take the wrong job, and then the right one becomes obvious. Maybe, like South Carolina teen Katie Stagliano, they're introduced to a need in the world and inspiration strikes.

Katie stumbled upon her purpose in the third grade. As part of a school project, she planted and cared for a cabbage seedling. Her passion was hard at work even before she realized what it was. She tended to the cabbage every day, making sure it was watered, fertilized,

and weeded. When deer threatened it, she and her grandfather built a cage to surround it. Her love and attention helped the cabbage grow to 40 pounds. (That's like four bowling balls!)

EMPOWERING KIDS

Katie's seedling came from Bonnie Plants, a company that sells vegetable and herb plants. They started their nationwide 3rd Grade Cabbage Plant Program in 1996 to encourage kids to get involved in gardening and growing their own food. One participating student in each state wins a $1,000 scholarship. Bonnie Plants has shipped more than 14 million seedlings over the life of the program and helped kids all over the country make an impact on health, hunger, and the environment.

This was no ordinary cabbage, so Katie felt that it needed an extraordinary home. She and her parents decided to donate it to a local soup kitchen, but they didn't just drop it off. Katie herself served her cabbage to a long line of people in need waiting for what might have been their only meal of the day. And in that moment, she found her purpose.

If one cabbage could help feed 275 people in her community, she could only imagine what one garden could do. So she approached her school about donating land and drumming up student volunteers for a community garden. She also reached out to Fields to Families, an organization that helps connect farmers to people in need, about her project. With a garden the size of a football field, student volunteers from kindergarten through 12th grade, and a Master Gardener from Fields to Families, Katie's Krops was born.

That one garden creates 3,000 pounds of fresh produce annually for people in need. But Katie didn't stop there. Her organization provides funding and support to kids all over the country to help them start their own community gardens. Today, she's helped create more than 100 gardens in 30 states. She also started a summer camp where

> **"SOME PEOPLE APPROACH AN ISSUE AND THINK, *THIS PROBLEM'S JUST TOO BIG, I CAN'T DO ANYTHING ABOUT IT.* BUT IT DOESN'T MATTER HOW SMALL YOUR ACTIONS ARE, YOU'RE MAKING A DIFFERENCE."**
>
> —KATIE STAGLIANO

kids can come to learn about growing techniques and food safety while forging friendships with other young growers.

When her local soup kitchen was forced to close, Katie also began organizing Katie's Krops Dinners at a local church. She and her fellow growers and friends harvest fresh produce and cook a healthy garden-to-table dinner that's free to more than 150 people in need once a month. (That's in addition to the produce the organization donates on a regular basis.)

Katie wasn't born knowing how to garden or that she wanted to help people. She didn't know she would uncover a passion for both. She just followed that little voice in her head that told her "this is important," and she put one foot in front of the other. Today, she is helping to end hunger in America, one cabbage plant at a time.

THROWING STARFISH

Once upon a time, a storm washed thousands of starfish onto a beach. Unable to find their way back to the water, the starfish wouldn't live through the day. A man walking along the beach saw a little girl throwing the starfish back into the ocean. He asked the girl why she would bother—there were thousands of starfish and only one of her. What difference could it make? She threw another one back in, smiled, and said, "It made a difference to that one!"

That well-known parable is the key to creating change. Problems like hunger or climate change are so overwhelming that most people don't know where to start. How can one person make a difference when millions are starving and storms are raging? Katie, like the little girl on the beach, took things one step at a time. She saw hunger in her own community, and she found a small way to help. Then she shared her idea with others, and together they're helping families in need around the country.

Imagine if the little girl on the beach had shared her simple idea—how many more starfish might she have helped?

EMMA GONZÁLEZ

GUN CONTROL ACTIVIST

BORN: 2000

- Survived the 2018 shooting at Marjory Stoneman Douglas High that killed 17
- Advocates for common-sense gun control and school safety
- Leading the way for her generation's involvement in politics

"WE ARE SPEAKING UP FOR THOSE WHO DON'T HAVE ANYONE LISTENING TO THEM, FOR THOSE WHO CAN'T TALK ABOUT IT JUST YET, AND FOR THOSE WHO WILL NEVER SPEAK AGAIN." –EMMA GONZÁLEZ

Whether you're a straight-A student or someone who regularly sleeps through science class, you probably have your fair share of school-related stress. Maybe you worry about what to wear, or whether you'll pass that math test. Maybe you're facing more serious problems, like bullying. But 18-year-old Emma González has made it her mission to ensure that students like you never have to worry about school shootings.

Between binge-watching Netflix and thinking about college, the bright and tenacious high school senior made a habit of standing up for what she believed in. When she decided her long, curly hair was too heavy for the Florida heat, she used a PowerPoint presentation to convince her parents to let her cut it all off. When Egypt began arresting its gay and transgender citizens, Emma advocated for them in her school paper as both a bisexual person and president of her high school's Gay-Straight Alliance club.

WHAT IS GUN CONTROL?

When people like Emma say they want "gun control," they mean they want a government body to keep track of and regulate guns, similar to the way the Motor Vehicle Commission tracks and regulates cars. They also want to ban some military-style guns (like the ones most often used in school shootings) so that they can't be purchased for personal use. Many countries—including Canada, Australia, and Germany—already have gun control laws, and shooting deaths in those countries have decreased dramatically as a result.

But Emma first made national headlines in the wake of the horrific Parkland, Florida, shooting at Marjory Stoneman Douglas High School. When an angry young man took the lives of 17 of her classmates and teachers, she chose to stand up for them and be their voice. Emma made her mission clear: "It should not be easier to purchase a gun than it is to obtain a driver's license, and military-grade weapons should not be accessible in civilian settings." She and fellow survivors have done news interviews and taken to social media to shine a light on the personal cost of America's gun laws, and to demand change.

The gun control debate has been raging for years, and it gets especially heated as more mass shootings take place. Many Americans believe that owning guns is their constitutional right, and that any move to regulate them is a step closer to disarming even law-abiding gun owners. At this point, however, two-thirds of all Americans—including a slight majority of gun owners—want stricter gun laws. But few people choose to get involved in politics and fight for what they want. Creating change is slow and difficult work, and the adults have dropped the ball.

That's why Emma's call to action is so powerful—she's inspiring her generation to pick up the ball and run with it toward a better future. She and her Stoneman Douglas classmates are channeling their shock and grief into creating a nationwide movement. During a fiery speech just days after the shooting, Emma said, "We are going to be the kids you read about in the textbooks. Not because we are going to be another statistic about mass shooting in America, but because we are going to be the last mass shooting.... We are going to change the law." And they're already making more progress than many adults who have tried before them. She and her fellow activists even made the cover of *Time* magazine on April 2, 2018, for sparking the #NeverAgain movement.

They are working hard to remind Americans that senators and congressmen are chosen *representatives* for the people in their

**MARCH FOR OUR LIVES** districts. (In other words, they work for *you*.) They are meeting with their representatives, demanding change, and encouraging young people around the country to do the same. They are driving home the importance of registering to vote and of voting in *every* election to help create that change.

They are also organizing marches across the country. The March for Our Lives on March 24, 2018, saw hundreds of thousands of people come together to demand that school safety become a priority in Washington, DC. During the rally, Emma read the names of each of the 17 Parkland shooting victims. She then stood in silence, staring fiercely into the massive crowd with tears rolling down her cheeks, for the remainder of 6 minutes and 20 seconds—the amount of time it took for the shooter to take the lives of the people she named.

The urge to fill a silence can become overwhelming in 10 seconds, let alone in more than 4 minutes. But Emma didn't break. She finished her speech by saying, "Fight for your lives before it is someone else's job" and walked off the stage. News outlets across the country called her speech powerful and brave, and one analyst called it "the loudest silence in the history of U.S. social protest." Without saying a word, Emma made the whole country feel her pain and her passion.

Active shooter drills are now as common as fire drills in schools across the country, but Emma wants to make them a thing of the past. She isn't sitting around, waiting for permission to make a difference. She's leading. She's helping people register to vote. She's organizing events and protests. She's proving that leaders can come from anywhere, including a Florida high school. Emma has seen the consequence of gun violence first hand and she is doing something about it.

LEADERS OF TOMORROW

First, Emma and her friends faced gunfire. Then they faced the loss of their classmates and teachers. Now, they are facing adults all over the country who dismiss them as too young and too emotional to know what they're talking about. Emma says that "Adults like us when we have strong test scores, but they hate us when we have strong opinions." But she's not backing down. She and her classmates have armed themselves with knowledge and their 1st Amendment rights, and they are leading the way in the fight against gun violence. The mission statement for their march reads, "Change is coming. And it starts now, inspired by and led by the kids who are our hope for the future. Their young voices will be heard." These brave, intelligent, and articulate teens are not letting their age stand in their way.

MAYA PENN

ENTREPRENEUR AND ENVIRONMENTALIST

BORN: 2000

- Created a line of eco-friendly clothing and accessories before she turned 13
- Donates a percentage of her profits to local charities
- Has given 3 TED Talks and received commendations, awards, and a publishing deal

"WOMEN AND GIRLS MUST EMPOWER EACH OTHER, SPEAK LIFE INTO EACH OTHER, AND LIFT EACH OTHER UP SO THAT THEY MAY LIFT UP HUMANITY." –MAYA PENN

Have you ever gotten in trouble for asking too many questions? Curiosity can bother some people, but it can also lead to amazing things. Alice followed hers to Wonderland and had the adventure of a lifetime. In our own world, 18-year-old Georgia native Maya Penn followed her curiosity and changed the way we do business.

Maya's first love was animation. She's been drawing since the moment she could hold a crayon in her hand. When she watched a TV program about animators (people who create cartoons), she knew that's what she wanted to

do with her life. But her second love, fashion, crept in when she was eight years old and took hold of her. She began making and selling headbands out of scraps of fabric she found around the house, and her business took off. By the age of 14, she was already earning more money annually than the average adult.

Soon after starting her business, she incorporated her third love: the environment. She says, "We live in

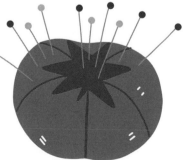

a big, diverse, and beautiful world, and that makes me even more passionate to save it." While doing research, she learned that many fabric dyes can be harmful to both humans and the planet. She decided then to use only eco-friendly materials (recycled fabrics or fabrics that are manufactured in an eco-conscious way). She also decided that a portion of her profits should give back to the world from which we take so much, so she donates 10 percent to local charities.

PARTNERS IN CURIOSITY

Luckily for Maya, her parents always encouraged her curiosity. When she expressed an interest in fashion, her mother taught her how to sew. When she was curious about technology, her father taught her how to take apart and rebuild a computer. Without their support, Maya may not have had the courage to act on her ideas.

If you're passionate about something, don't be afraid to seek out like-minded people. Ask a teacher to mentor you, or your friends to help you. Sure, you can go it alone. But everything is easier when you have a little support.

Like Tavi Gevinson (see page 99), Maya is bravely multipassionate. Instead of focusing on just one business avenue, she named her company the all-encompassing "Maya's Ideas." Right now, her website (which she coded and designed herself) offers eco-friendly clothing and accessories. But she's giving herself room to explore and grow in whatever direction she chooses. In fact, she's so passionate about following her curiosity that she gave a TED Talk on the subject (one of three, so far) that's been viewed more than 1.5 million times! (TED talks are inspiring lectures that are shared online under the slogan, "ideas worth spreading.")

While this might seem like a perfectly logical concept—especially for a 17-year-old—we've only recently come to accept multipassionate people like Tavi and Maya. Conventional wisdom used to tell us that you had to pick one path and stick to it for the rest of your life. You were a doctor, or a teacher, or a veterinarian, and any pursuits outside of your chosen career were called *hobbies*. Changing jobs used to be considered flaky, and changing careers was almost unheard of.

The old business model was also focused on profits over principles. But Maya, like many business owners these days, thinks you can have both. She also thinks it's important to try, saying, "I may be one person, but

"BE CREATIVE, BE CURIOUS, AND WATCH AS YOUR AWESOMENESS IS UNLEASHED." —MAYA PENN

the smallest actions can lead to the biggest change." Businesses like hers recognize a shift in society. People are starting to choose ethical and sustainable products from charitable brands over what's cheap and convenient.

YOU GOT THIS!

People like Maya are transforming the way we think about work. By successfully pursuing all of her passions—animation, entrepreneurship, and environmentalism—she is proving that you don't have to choose. As Maya says, "It's important to encourage girls to follow their passion, and to be changemakers and creative thinkers. They can do anything if they just believe in themselves." And as traditional jobs disappear, forging your own path becomes the smart move. Curiosity and flexibility are superpowers in a world that keeps changing.

A VERY SWEET 16

Maya's innovative and entrepreneurial spirit caught the attention of some pretty important people in 2016. That year, she received a commendation from President Barack Obama for outstanding achievement in environmental stewardship and the Coretta Scott King A.N.G.E.L. (Advancing Nonviolence through Generations of Exceptional Leadership) Award. In addition, Oprah Winfrey made her a member of the Supersoul 100, which is a group of "awakened leaders who are using their voices and talents to elevate humanity." And if all of that isn't enough, 2016 was also the year Maya published her inspiring book, *You Got This!: Unleash Your Awesomeness, Find Your Path, and Change Your World.*

Can you imagine a better way to celebrate your 16th birthday than by changing the world?

JAZZ JENNINGS

ADVOCATE FOR TRANSGENDER RIGHTS

BORN: 2000

- One of the youngest people to be formally recognized as transgender
- Fought for her right to use the girls' bathroom and play on the girls' soccer team
- Has dedicated her life to advocating for trans kids

"BE WHO YOU ARE AND SAY WHAT YOU FEEL, BECAUSE THOSE WHO MIND DON'T MATTER AND THOSE WHO MATTER DON'T MIND." –DR. SEUSS

Has anyone ever told you to "just be yourself"? It's important advice, but it's also easier said than done sometimes. Maybe you're afraid people will think you're a nerd for loving *Star Wars*. Or maybe you've stopped smiling because you're self-conscious about your braces. When those fears come up, just remember that Dr. Seuss quote. Those are the words Jazz Jennings turns to when she starts to worry about what others think.

From the moment she learned to talk, Jazz made it clear to her parents that she was different. Jazz herself knew even earlier

than that. She says, "Ever since I could form coherent thoughts, I knew I was a girl trapped inside a boy's body. There was never any confusion in my mind. The confusing part

WHAT IS GENDER DYSPHORIA?

Gender dysphoria is the scientific diagnosis given to people who are transgender. It means that they feel deeply and constantly uncomfortable with the gender they were born with. Instead, they identify with the opposite gender, often feeling like they're in the wrong body, or that who they are inside doesn't match what they look like outside. Imagine how you would feel if you woke up tomorrow in someone else's body, and only you knew the truth.

was why no one else could see what was wrong." When she was just three years old, a psychiatrist confirmed what Jazz knew: she was transgender.

At first, the confirmation was a relief to Jazz and her parents. There was a name for what she felt. She wasn't the only one who felt this way. Jazz's parents were incredibly supportive and allowed her to fully transition when she turned five, so that she could have a fresh start in her new school. But Jazz still had an uphill battle ahead of her.

DOES IT REALLY MATTER?

Because she has had to deal with so many big, real-world issues, Jazz learned that all of the drama and gossip of middle school and high school weren't worth her time. Her motto is, "Is it going to matter in twenty years? Yes or no?" If the answer is no, she moves on.

Many people aren't as understanding as the Jenningses about what it means to be transgender. Some think it's a choice or a phase, that a girl like Jazz is just a boy playing dress-up. The truly unkind ones call her a "freak." But from a young age, Jazz learned to fight for her right to live life as her true self. At eight years old, she began a two-year-long battle to be allowed to play for the girls' soccer team. When she was nine, she sent a video plea to President Obama to be allowed to use the girls' bathrooms. These are the kind of simple, everyday things we often take for granted, but that trans kids have to fight for.

Jazz believes that educating the public is the best way to defend against the kind of bullying and ignorance she's encountered. That's why she and her family never shied away from the spotlight. Jazz gave her first of many interviews when she was six years old—to no less than famous journalist Barbara Walters! Her YouTube channel, where she shares her very normal life as a teenage girl, led to not one but two similarly themed television shows. She regularly attends and speaks at events as a champion of the LGBTQ community. She was also named one of *Time* magazine's 25 Most Influential Teens in 2014.

Jazz has spent so much of her life helping people understand trans issues and letting them get to know her as a normal (though very smart, brave, and articulate) young woman. Why does she do it? She answers, "When I leave, I want the world to be in a better state than when I arrived. I have made it my mission to contribute to that change in any way I can." And it seems like she finds new ways every day.

Being different can be scary. But at the end of the day, the only opinion of you that matters is your own. So, you do you! And if you help others feel included and understood whenever you can, you too will have left the world in a better state than when you arrived.

"I'M WILLING TO SACRIFICE MY PRIVACY IF IT MEANS MAKING A DIFFERENCE AND HELPING OTHER PEOPLE OUT THERE WHO MIGHT BE STRUGGLING." —JAZZ JENNINGS

WHEN PASSION MEETS PURPOSE

Jazz, who has always loved mermaids, started handcrafting her own tails to swim with when she was eight years old. At thirteen, she decided to use her tail-making skills to raise money for the TransKids Purple Rainbow Foundation, an organization created by her family to educate the public and support transgender children. Each tail sold was handmade from premium silicone (to give the wearer a real mermaid experience) and airbrushed in beautiful colors.

Have you ever thought about combining something you love to do with a cause you believe in? You could share your love of reading with the little ones at your library's story time. Or sell homemade cookies to raise money for the animal shelter. There are plenty of ways to make a difference and enjoy doing it!

ABOUT THE AUTHOR & ILLUSTRATOR

JENNIFER CALVERT is a writer and editor with dozens of credits in nonfiction publishing. When she isn't highlighting the accomplishments of incredible young women, you can find her curled up with a book and a cat in New Jersey.

VESNA ASANOVIC is an illustrator living in Toronto. She holds a BDes from Ontario College of Art and Design. She works primarily digitally with a particular interest in bright, bold colors and graphic shapes. In her free time you can find Vesna drawing in her sketchbook on a sunny patio.